Singing
to the
Sound

Singing
to the
Sound

Visions of Nature,
Animals & Spirit

BRENDA PETERSON

NEWSAGE PRESS

SINGING TO THE SOUND:
Visions of Nature, Animals & Spirit

Copyright © 2000 by Brenda Peterson
ISBN 0-939165-41-4

NewSage Press
PO Box 607
Troutdale, OR 97060-0607
503-695-2211

web site: http://www.newsagepress.com
email: info@newsagepress.com

Cover Design by Christine Lamb
Book Design by Patricia Keelin
Cover Photo © Chris Huss

Apprenticeship to Animal Play and *Listening to the Sea Breathing*
first appeared in the anthology *Intimate Nature: The Bond Between
Women and Animals.*

Printed in the United States on recycled paper with soy ink.

Distributed in the United States and Canada by
Publishers Group West 800-788-3123

        Library of Congress Cataloging-in-Publication Data
Peterson, Brenda, 1950-
  Singing to the sound : visions of nature, animals, and spirit / Brenda
Peterson.-- 1st ed.
     p. cm.
  ISBN 0-939165-41-4 (softcover : alk. paper) --
  1. Nature. 2. Natural history. I. Title.
QH81.P48 2000
508--dc21

00-036061

For Puget Sound,
daily companion and watery muse

Contents

Acknowledgments

This book owes much of its birth to the inspired editing and vision of my NewSage Press publisher Maureen R. Michelson. I will always be grateful for her support and steadiness during this book-making, which seems, with every book, more and more a mystery.

I would also like to acknowledge and thank Vanessa Adams and Lesa Quale for their editorial assistance. My dear friend and artist Christine Lamb designed this glorious cover with her good heart and superb eye. NewSage Press designer Patricia Keelin created the handsome interior of this book with a great gift for attention to detail. My wonderful and wise agent Elizabeth Wales has given me more than astute advice; she has given me a future. To Susan Biskeborn, my first reader for almost two decades, I give lifelong gratitude—I just don't know what my writing would be without her weekly guidance, loyalty, and insight. And to my enduring friend and sister writer Linda Hogan I am grateful for good counsel, the example of her own wise work in the world, and companionable "nagging" to always do my best.

John and Micah McCarty, Alberta Thompson, of the Makah tribe have been kind enough to open their homes to me and I hope in this book to return their generosity and trust. My trusted editor at *The Seattle Times* over the past six years, Jim Vesely, has supported and offered me excellent, timely advice. To Dr. Toni Frohoff, my marine mammal expert and ally on many adventures, I owe deep thanks for reading at the last minute and kindly correcting. And I am very glad to share the weekly dialogue on the natural world with my wonderful students. I would also like to acknowledge the good work for wildlife of Joan Moody, Gerry Erickson of Defenders of Wildlife, Paul Joslin of Alaska Wildlife Alliance, Bobbie Holaday, Founder of Preserve Arizona's Wolves, Stan Butler of Whales Alive, Will Anderson of PAWS, Dr. Paul Spong and Helena Symond of OrcaLab, Ken and Kelly Balcomb of the Center for Whale Research, and Naomi Rose of HSUS. These are the people in the front lines who make a new century of wildlife restoration actually happen. I am also grateful to John and Adele Caton of Clayquot Wilderness Lodge in Tofino, B.C. who gave me shelter to write and research. And to Qaamina of the Ahousat First Nations who was our gray whale watch guide, I am thankful for your courage and vision of a new world in which humans and animals are kin.

In abiding acknowledgment of my neighbors who share this blessed beach, Bill McHalffey, Eve Anthony, and Joyce Russo.

And I am deeply grateful to my mother, whose own curiosity about the world taught me to tell stories; and to my father, whose lifetime of wildlife work inspires my own.

"What would the world be, once bereft
Of wet and wildness?
Let them be left,
O let them be left, wildness and wet;

— Gerard Manley Hopkins
"Inversnaid"

The Way of Water

Faithful Rain

If landscape is character, then Northwesterners are most like water. We are shaped by the voluptuous shores and salt tides of Puget Sound, the deep currents of the Columbia, Salmon, and Snake rivers. Northwesterners have always been water folk, shaped by this Sound and also by the sounds of rapid rivers and dousing rains. Our tales are syncopated with rhythms of tide and wind, cries of seagulls, osprey, and eagles, the mystical breath of whales, and grieving arpeggios of foghorns. Northwesterners are held back from falling off the proverbial edge of the world by a Pacific coastline whose nurturing rain forests and rocky peninsulas face the sea like guardians.

Our intimacy with water is crucial to understanding our Northwest character; we are more changed by the environment than it is by us. Once, a convention of New Yorkers visited

Seattle. On the harbor cruise to Blake Island, birthplace of Chief Sealth (Seattle), for a salmon feast hosted by Native Americans to re-create the first salmon bake and potlatch ceremonies that defined tribal life here for thousands of years, the tourists commented that everything seemed in slow motion.

"We've had to shift gears," said one New Yorker, somewhat anxiously. "Everything's so laid back. Maybe it's all those negative ions in the atmosphere."

Another visitor said, "How do you stand traffic jams on those floating bridges. Can't they just pave a part of Lake Washington?"

Finally, a rather pensive, bespectacled literary agent remarked, "Now I know why Seattle is single-handedly keeping New York's book business alive. You have to go inside in all this gray and wet. I feel like I'm dreaming."

"Must be why Seattle has espresso carts on every corner and some of the world's best coffee." Someone laughed. "It's to keep yourselves awake!"

When we try to spell out our "rainy day people" intimacies to outsiders, they cannot believe that we actually *enjoy* living for many months aswirl in great, flowing gowns of gray mist. To survive here without the daily illumination of sunlight, we must have an inner life bright with hidden worlds.

Northwest Coast Natives tell stories of sea creatures and underwater tribes that "shape-shift" into humans then return to the original People—the animals. For example, the Salmon People are an underwater tribe who also spend a season on land; the whales and seals can metamorphose into humans as easily as the ever-present mist and clouds change shape. Many

Northwest coast tribes tell of merpeople, part human, part mammal, who mediate between the worlds to keep a watery balance. One of the most common gods was called "Changer." Many Native tribes began their mythologies with water— floods and seas creating what we now call The People. A Skagit myth details this beginning, when Changer decided "to make all the rivers flow only one way" and that "there should be bends in the rivers, so that there would be eddies where the fish could stop and rest. Changer decided that beasts should be placed in the forests. Human beings would have to keep out of their way."

According to the Wasco Indians along the Columbia River, the tribe knew long before the white people came to settle at Alki Point, in 1851, that a change was coming. As told in Ella E. Clark's classic *Indian Legends of the Pacific Northwest*, one of the Wasco elders dreamed that "white people with hair on their faces will come from the rising sun." The strangers were prophesied to bring with them "iron birds that could fly" and "something—if you just point it at anything moving, that thing will fall down and die." They also brought new tools such as axes, hatchets, and stoves. Along with this new technology, the white people brought a philosophy of individual ownership of the land.

The Native Americans knew that the land could never be owned, just as it was impossible to section off the vast winding lengths of the emerald-clear body of Puget Sound. Even now, after more than a century of non-Indian dominance, Puget Sound property rights ebb and flow according to the tides, not the set boundaries of so-called landowners. Our ownership of Northwest land is called into daily question by changing tides.

Northwesterners not only reckon with water shaping our physical boundaries, but also our heavens. Rain is a Northwest native. One recent winter, we had twenty-seven inches of rain in three months and mudslides are now as familiar as side streets. Northwesterners live like slowly drowning people. We are well aware of the predictions that in the next millennium our Pacific Rim shores will sink from the volcanic *tsunami* waves into an Atlantis-like abyss. Our famous rainfall is perhaps all that shelters us from the massive population and industrial exploitations of nearby California. The rain is so omnipresent, especially between late October and even into June, that most Northwesterners disdain umbrellas, the true sign of any tourist.

One must be rather fluid to live underwater; one must learn to flow with a pulse greater than one's own. A tolerance for misting gray days means an acceptance that life itself is not black and white, but in between. If the horizons outside one's window are not sharply defined but ease into a sky intimately merged with sea and soft landscape, then perhaps shadows, both personal and collective, are not so terrifying. After all, most of the year Northwesterners can't even see their own literal shadows cast on the ground. We live inside the rain shadow. We tolerate edges and differences in people and places perhaps because our landscape blends and blurs as it embraces.

Widely acclaimed Port Angeles poet Tess Gallagher tells it this way: "It is a faithful rain. You feel it has some allegiance to the trees and the people.... It brings an ongoing thoughtfulness to their faces, a meditativeness that causes them to fall silent for long periods, to stand at their windows looking out at nothing in particular. The people walk in the rain as within some spirit they wish not to offend with resistance."

We pride ourselves on living within nature's laws, on listening to our environment before it is irreparably lost and silenced. It is, after all, here in the Northwest where the few last nurturing old-growth forests still stand, where people fight fiercely to preserve them for future generations. Here is also where the country's last salmon still spawn. But for all their strong conservation of nature, there are signs that even the "Rainy-Day People" are facing growing environmental challenges.

Oil spills blacken our beaches, and many species of salmon are endangered; gray whales are found on their migrating courses belly-up from pollution in Puget Sound. More than one-third of the Sound's tidelands and submerged marine beds surveyed have been contaminated. A March 2000 report on Puget Sound's health showed that the region's pollution, loss of habitat, and development are taking a heavy toll on the environment. In addition, the U.S Supreme Court dealt a disappointing blow to Washington State's protection of Puget Sound by superceding the state's more stringent oil tanker regulations, first adopted after the Exxon *Valdez* spill, by allowing less rigorous federal standards.

Some people are trying to help. For instance, The Puget Sound Alliance, a local program to protect Puget Sound, employs a full-time "Sound keeper" who patrols the shores checking reports of pollution. There is the highly acclaimed whale museum and its staff in Friday Harbor, who have been studying the transient and resident pods of orcas in the San Juan Islands for many years. People for Puget Sound and other local grass-roots organizations are working to protect this beloved inland sea for the future.

Such bio-regionalism and environmental commitment runs strong in the Northwest. The 1999 protests in Seattle during the World Trade Organization's meeting showed the world just how strongly we value nature. Peaceful WTO protesters, dressed as endangered sea turtles and butterflies, marched against the WTO's history of putting free-trade above environmental concerns. Other protesters raised issues of corporate deforestation, water pollution, the illegal trade in endangered animals, and child labor. These massive and highly visible WTO protests in Seattle put the Northwest in the spotlight as a future, international leader in protecting our natural world.

Just as Northwesterners claim closeness with their natural world, so too are we close to our own history. Compared with the Native tribes, we settlers are young. Our history here is only two hundred years, compared with thousands of years of Skagit, Suquamish, Muckleshoot, Okanogan, Makah, and multitudinous other tribal roots. Some of these Indian myths calmly predict that "the human beings will not live on this Earth forever." This is an agreement between Raven, Mink, Coyote, and who the Skagits call "Old Creator." The prophecy predicts that human beings "will stay only for a short time. Then the body will go back to the Earth and the spirit back to the spirit world." The possibility of this simple ebb and flow of our human tribe seems more resonant here—here where the animals interchange lives with the humans, where the mists can transform entire settlements and skyscrapers into low-hung cloudbanks.

Our human conceits carry less weight in this watery world. Perhaps this is why during the first days of the Persian Gulf War, as during those seventy-two hours of the failed coup in the Soviet Union, it was remarked that there were more fishing boats on Puget Sound than usual. It is typically Northwestern that this gone-fishing-while-the-world-falls-apart attitude prevails while in other areas of the country the population is transfixed by CNN. It is not that Northwesterners aren't deeply involved, it's just that nature can be an antidote to such strong doses of terror.

Even the first Native Americans were known not so much as warriors but as fishermen. While there were territory battles, there was also a diversity and abundance of food that contrasted sharply with the Southwest tribal struggles over scarce resources. Amidst this plentitude, Northwest art flour-ished—so did storytelling.

Nature can also remind us that there are other mysteries at work in the world, which might hold more power than our own. There is a strong Asian influence here in the Pacific Northwest. Seattle's expansive harbor is a gateway to the Orient, and the strong, graceful pull of that more feminine culture is felt here. In fact, the classic *Tao Te Ching*, by the ancient Chinese master Lao Tzu, could well be a description of the Puget Sound landscape and character—we are flexible and fluid. And more hopeful. Li Po, ancient Taoist sage, writes:

Since water still flows, though we cut it with swords
And sorrow returns, though we drown it with wine,
Since the world can in no way answer to our craving,
I will loosen my hair tomorrow and take to a fishing boat.

If water is our Northwest character and rainy reverie our temperament, it follows that those of us who stay long in the Pacific Northwest must develop an inner life to sustain us through the flow of so many changing gray days. We must awaken even though it may still seem like night and recognize another radiance. This means that ambition is not only an outward thrust toward manipulating our environment; ambition may also be an inner journey, not to change but to understand the often unexplored territory within, what poet Rilke calls "the dark light." Are we a more mystical region and people? Let's just say the climate is there and so is the "faithful rain."

Singing to the Sound

For two decades now I have cleaved to the misting, mysterious shores of Washington's Puget Sound, far-flung in the Pacific Northwest. The Salish Indians call Puget Sound *Whulge*, which truly sounds more like this Sound with its deluge of mighty gales and intimate, watery whisperings. My beach studio, with its walls of salt-splattered windows, its wind-tunnel whoosh and clatter, its precarious perch several stories above the high-tide splashing of the Sound is like living inside an aquarium. Except here, humans go about our daily lives encased in glass, while sea gulls, bald eagles, Dall's porpoises, harbor seals, orca pods, and an occasional meandering, migrating gray whale are the observers.

Sometimes I believe they are, since seals are known to fix on a familiar landmark on shore and navigate their deep, fishing dives. Perhaps marine mammals who surface to spy on our human activities consider our shore-clinging structures to be alive like an undersea coral reef city. We land creatures slip in and out of our houses, hide for long hours as if we were moray eels or tropical fish with our flickering bright yellow and red rain slickers.

So my daily meditations inside this weather-beaten studio are most often centered on water. And my air-filled aquarium apartment beached here on the Sound is the closest I can get to my childhood dream of living inside a diving bell at 50,000 leagues under the sea.

The Sound is an inland sea—cold, fertile, fabled. Its lovely lengths embrace our islands and peninsulas like a green dragon that coils north from Seattle, entwines its fresh water with the salty Straits of Georgia and Juan de Fuca, and finally comes to lick at the docks of Vancouver and Victoria. Our Sound is studded with fjords and long archipelagoes. Sometimes gazing out my window at Bainbridge, Vashon, and Blake islands, I imagine they are breaching whales, blowing mists of lavender-gray geysers.

Our abundant, defining coast holds us all together with its cadences of water and weather. Sometimes we feel so hidden by marine fog and darkening showers that we wonder if our far-off territory is truly isolated from the remaining, mostly landlocked sprawl of North America.

When I describe for my far-away friends the Northwest's subtle shades of weather—from gloaming skies of "high-gray" to "low-gray" with violet streaks like the water's delicate aura—they wonder if my brain and body have, indeed, become water-logged. Yet still, I find myself praising the solace and privacy of fine, silver drizzle, the comforting cloaks of salt, mold, moss, and fog, the secretive shelter of cedar and clouds.

Whether it's in the Florida Keys, along the rocky Maine coast, within the Gulf of Mexico's warm curves, on the brave Outer Banks; or, for those who nestle near inland seas such as the brine-steeped Great Salt Lake or the Midwest's Great Lakes—water is alive and in relationship with those of us who are blessed with such a world-shaping, yet abiding, intimate ally.

Every day, I am moved by the double life of water—her power and her humility. But most of all, I am grateful for the partnership of this great body of inland sea. Living by water, I am never alone. Just as water has sculpted soil and canyon, it also molds my own living space, and every story I tell.

My studio's battered teak desk is sun-blistered and rain-swept from summer winds blowing sea mists in through window screens. It looks like salvage washed ashore off some nineteenth-century shipwreck. Writing out here on the glass-paneled porch, with no baseboard heating, I wear a black-knit cap, goose down vest, wool mittens with no fingers, and an afghan or Siamese Manx cat draped across my knees.

At the end of the workday, it feels as if I have been sailing outdoors for hours. A mahogany rocking chair and several pine bookcases in my aquarium office look waterlogged because the damp winds of winter bluster right through the waterfront windows like a loquacious guest. I am lucky. I like the whistling sound of the windy monologue that accompanies the unceasing syncopation of the sea. Waves are a second language to me. And whenever someone telephones, my voice may be drowned out by sea gulls crying. If I'm lounging in the bathtub, I hear the raucous dinosaur-call of the great blue heron through the air vent above as if that great-winged bird is dive-bombing my little bubble-bath lagoon. At night, reading in bed by my stained-glass blue water lamp with its full-spectrum light, I close my eyes and simply listen to the stories told by sounds, as if all the silkies and sea sprites are singing me chanties to sleep.

Living so close to this vital, inland sea and all her creatures lends my home expansiveness and balance. My waterfront studio's decor is an extension of the beach as if designed by mermaids. Lining each long windowsill are seashells, drift-wood, a Chambered Nautilus, and black, bejeweled barnacles. All my plants, from desert aloe vera to humid Norfolk pine, have somehow found themselves draped with dried seaweed. There are binoculars for handy viewing whenever my resting eye catches sight of a seal, river otter, or eagle diving down for salmon. In the hope that passing marine mammals will recognize a land-legged ally, I hang small stained-glass medallions of orcas and dolphins in the window. Facing these wide windows hangs a Makah drum painted with a thunderbird, whale, and serpents by Makah master carver Spencer McCarty; this Native drum was given to me by my friends to auspiciously mark my birthday, which fell that year on August 8, 1988.

I imagine my little kitchen is a galley. Turquoise tiles the color of Hawaiian waters adorn the walls with a few yellow trim tiles to remind me of sun—which is usually no more than a faint rumor here. Over the kitchen stove there is a favorite children's book poster, *A Swim Through the Sea*, with Seamore the Seahorse and "many munching manatees." There are also cooking essentials: a copper mold pan in the shape of a leaping salmon, a bronze dolphin bottle opener, and a midnight blue-glazed teakettle with a whale's tail for a handle. Orca and bottlenose dolphin magnets breach right on my refrigerator, holding up a family album of photos, both human and cetacean.

When it doesn't smell of spicy tea, basil, or nutmeg, my kitchen offers the bittersweet scent of mold compliments of brine and kelp, and sometimes the pungent waft of neighboring fish swimming right by my skillet. And one spring evening, as I was washing dishes, I glanced out the window to marvel at a giant gray whale, graceful tail flukes waving as it migrated.

There is a bond and a balance when one counts as neighbors the marine kinfolk and seabirds who share our beach. Except for one neighbor, who hired an animal control agency to trap several river otters she found rolling on her lawn, many of us here on Puget Sound embrace the other animals who make our houses seem alive, our families extended. In fact, those otter traps were destroyed as soon as they were discovered. And within a month, the river otters returned to our backyard beach, even going so far as to lazily lounge and sunbathe on two sailboats anchored out in the Sound.

For those of us who choose the companionship of water, there is always the longing to give something back, to grow even closer to this other body of water, like the elusive desire for a lover. We water folk are possessive, protective, and passionate. I will never forget witnessing one luminous Solstice and Christmas celebration—where else? But on the beach. It was a night that will always define for me both the hope of a New Year, a new millennium, and the prospect of reciprocity between humans and nature.

The December tide was low and the moon full when hundreds of people huddled together in circles around a bonfire on Alki Beach. Christmas boats strung with red and gold lights glided across the ebony Sound like winter bobsleds skimming black ice. In the perfect, chill air, liquid music from the Christmas boats carried across the accompanying waves. As we celebrated these darkest days of the year, our spirits and breaths were visible in bright puffs. We sang Solstice songs to summon back the wayward sun. Addressing ourselves to angels and passing harbor seals, we raised a chorus of "Angels We Have Heard on High." The bonfire glowed like a small sun settled on the beach and illuminated our faces. Our boots sunk deep in wet, winter sand and although the night was freezing, we sang our "Glor-or-or-or-or-or-ria!" in perfect synch with the surf.

I wondered if any sea lions raised their whiskered snouts to listen to our glad song. Were gray whales passing on their migration to winter breeding grounds trying to decipher our gleeful vocalizations? Did jellyfish and seals float a little easier near our shores because we were singing to them? How long had it been since an entire tribe of people made joyful noises of song on this stretch of sand? As we sang at the top of our voices, the children ran circles around the bonfire and stopped to adorn themselves with seaweed and shells.

Harmonies of surf, wave, and human voices held me close and I remembered a childhood story—an Indian girl plays atop the round, hard shell of a tortoise that is really the whole world. One day the great Grandmother Turtle wakes up, stretches out her sleepy head, and discovers the little girl on her big back. Will the turtle shake the girl off as a parasite or let her continue living on top of her shell? The Grandmother Turtle and little girl make a simple bargain: the girl can stay on the turtle's sturdy, round back if she will always remember to sing to Grandmother Turtle as she sleeps. If the singer ever stops so does the symbiosis.

So I sing here to the Sound, to *Whulge* and her multi-tudinous sea creatures whose lives accompany mine. Living by water restores my sense of balance and natural rhythm—the ebb and flow of high and low tides, so like the rise and fall of everyday life. Wind, water, waves are not simply a backdrop to my life; they are steady companions. And that is the grace, the gift of inviting nature to live inside my home. Like a Chambered Nautilus I spin out my days, drifting and dreaming, nurtured by marine mists, like another bright shell on the beach, balancing on the back of a greater body.

Bread Upon the Waters

"Seagulls memorize your face," the old man called out to me as he strode past on his daily walk. I stood on the sea wall feeding the flock of gray-and-white gulls who also make this Puget Sound beach their home. "They know their neighbors." He tipped his rather rakish tweed motoring cap and kept walking fast. "Can't let the heartbeat stop," he explained.

I meet this man many days on the beach. We rarely talk; we perform our simple chores: I feed the seagulls and say prayers, he keeps his legs and his heart moving. But between us there is an understanding that these tasks are as important as anything else in our lives; maybe they even keep us alive. Certainly our relationship with each other and with this windswept Northwest beach is more than a habit. It is a bond, an unspoken treaty we've made with the territory we call home.

For ten years I have migrated from beach shack to cabin, moving along the shore like the Native tribes that once encircled all of Puget Sound. But unlike the first people who loved this wild, serpentine body of cold water, my encampments have changed with the whim of my landlords rather than with the seasons. Somehow mixed up in my blood of Seminole, Swede, and French-Canadian Indian is the belief that one may never truly own land. Ownership implies possession. As much as I revere this inland sea, she will never belong to me. Why not, then, belong to her?

Belong. As a child the word mesmerized me. Because my father's forestry work moved us every other year—from southern piney woods to soaring Montana spruce to High Sierra fir—the landscape seemed in motion. To *be long* in one place was to take deep root like other settled folk, or like the trees themselves. After I have lived a long life on this beach, I hope that someone might someday say, "She belonged here," as much as the purple starfish that cling to rock crevices covered in algae fur.

The Hopi Indians of Arizona believe that our daily rituals and prayers literally keep this world spinning on its axis. For me, feeding the seagulls is one of those everyday prayers. They caw welcome, their wings almost touching me as they sail low over my shoulders, then hover overhead, midair. Sometimes if it's been raining, their feathers flick water droplets onto my face like sprinklings of holy water. The brave fliers swoop over the sea and back to catch the bread in their beak inches above my hand. Then the cacophonies of choir-gulls crying and crows *kok-kok-ing* as my special sidearm pitch sends tortillas whizzing through the air, a few of them skipping across the waves like flour Frisbees.

I am not the only neighbor who feeds these gulls. For the past three years, two afternoons a week, a green taxi pulled alongside the beach. From inside, an ancient woman, her back bent like the taut arch of a crossbow, leaned out of the car window. She called in a clear, tremulous soprano. The seagulls recognized the sun-wrinkled, almost blind face she raised to them. She smiled and said to the taxi driver, "They know I'm here."

It was always the same driver, the same ritual—a shopping bag full of day-old bread donated by a local baker. "She told me she used to live by the sea," the driver explained to me once. "She don't remember much else about her life... not her children, not her husband." Carefully the driver tore each bread slice into four squares the way the woman requested. "Now she can't hardly see these birds. But she hears them and she smells the sea. Calls this *taking her medicine*."

Strong medicine, the healing salt and mineral sea this old woman took into her body and soul twice a week. She lived in the nursing home at the top of our hill, and every time I saw the familiar ambulance go by I prayed it not be for Our Lady of the Gulls.

One fall, when wild hurricanes shook the South and drought seized the Northwest, the old woman stopped coming to our beach. I waited for her all autumn, but the green taxi with its delighted passenger never called again. I took to adding two weekly afternoon feedings to my own morning schedule. These beach meetings are more mournful, in memory of the old woman who didn't remember her name, whose name I never knew, who remembered only the gulls.

Not long afterward my landlady called with the dreaded refrain: "House sold, must move on." I walked down to the beach and opened my arms to the gulls. With each bread slice I said a prayer that Puget Sound would keep me near her. One afternoon I got the sudden notion to drive down the Sound. There I found a cozy white cottage for rent, a little beach house that belongs to an old man who has lived on this promontory since the 1940s. A stroke had sent him to a nursing home, and the rent from his cottage will pay for his care.

Before I moved one stick of furniture into the house, I stood on the beach and fed the gulls in thanksgiving. They floated above my head; I felt surrounded by little angels. Then I realized that these were the very same gulls from two miles down the beach near my old home. There was that bit of fish line wrapped around a familiar webbed foot, that wounded wing, and the distinct markings of a young gray gull, one of my favorite high fliers.

Who knows whether the old man was right? The seagulls may have memorized my face and followed me. But I had also, quite without realizing it, memorized them. And I knew then that I was no newcomer here, a nomad blown by changeable autumn winds. It is not to any house, but to this beach that I have bonded. I belong alongside this rocky inlet with its salt tides, its pine-tiered, green islands, and its gulls who remember us even when we've forgotten ourselves.

Spill

One summer morning as I sat in my small waterfront studio, perusing the calm waters of the Sound, I suddenly noticed a stream of sickly white runoff spewing into the clear waves. A chalky cloud bloomed on the beach and the seabirds scattered with squawks of alarm. I ran out into the hallway to find my neighbors already on the alert.

"The Department of Ecology and King County Parks both say they'll send someone out here within the hour," my neighbor Lisa called as she waited by the phone. Her husband Victor and I and our apartment manager Bill clambered over giant driftwood down to the beach where we saw a disturbing sight; filmy, white rivulets running into Puget Sound through a wide culvert.

"Oh, no," Victor said, "this is where the otters swim down to fish on the beach." He scooped up a sample of the unnatural runoff and scowled, "Looks really toxic." We both followed Bill's gaze up the hillside trying to track the watershed.

"Construction," Bill groaned, nodding to a new house halfway up the hill. "Let's check it out."

Victor found the culprit, a painting contractor whom he discovered casually washing gallons of white paint into a stream uphill from our beach. Calmly, Victor and Bill interrupted the commercial dumping. In his soft, school teacher's voice, Victor said, "You know, sir, the paint you're dumping into this little creek is polluting the stream and spilling down into the Sound itself."

"Oh," the contractor responded, looking abashed but not ashamed. "I was just washing out my truck where I spilled some... uh, paint."

Victor paused as if figuring out how to teach this adult a lesson every one of his school children knows by heart. Then Bill, a geologist who could also double as a wrestler, looked the painter square in the eye and said quietly, "No, sir. That paint's been flowing for over two hours. You should see what a mess you've made in the Sound."

The contractor turned away at last a little chagrined. "Oh, well... it's not oil base..." and he faded off. At least he stopped dumping the paint.

We returned to the beach and waited for the end of the pale trail to trickle out of the culvert. Watching the white cloud spill foam and filter into the waves, we wondered how many other neighborhoods that contractor had polluted, casually and with no sense of connection to our natural waterways. In the Northwest, these fragile, intricate watershed systems still spawn precious salmon, nourish backyard gardens, and shelter great blue herons. A toxic spill can be disastrous, even on this small scale. Could the paint, we worried, have poisoned the river otters who frequented our culvert?

As it turned out, our fears were relieved. The next week I sat on my backyard beach with my friend Marlene, who was born and reared on these shores. We heard a swoosh and thump and saw a small otter, her dark fur slick and gleaming, hopping on her belly and back flippers across barnacles and beach rocks to glide gracefully into the Sound. The frisky otter chittered and splashed before she suddenly dived and came up with a fat flounder flapping between her teeth. We clapped and the otter studied us, then hopped back up the beach, pausing to shake out her fur before disappearing into the culvert. We were relieved to see the otter swim upstream through that pipe that had so recently spilled paint—a reprieve from disaster.

Splashed across my kitchen table was *The Seattle Times* photo of a Prince William Sound loon, its fierce plumage slicked with the black slime of the largest oil spill ever to touch our far Northwest shores. Defiant, doomed, the loon's red eye gazed up and held mine; my eyes blurred as I gave way to the shame, rage, and helplessness I felt in March 1989 over the Exxon tanker *Valdez's* spill into what was once considered "safe" waters.

Nothing is safe now. Not the sea otters sprawled across dark shores; not the ducks and living birds frozen because their oil-soaked down could no longer insulate them; not the golden and bald eagles and peregrine falcons who starved slowly, their intestines destroyed by their grim feast of blackened wildlife. Even ashore, the deer, dependent on sea kelp, joined the oil spill's cull.

The safety and strict containment promised by the oil industry now seems as hollow as the bomb drills of the 1950s. And whether we're Alaskans who believed the oil industry's promises or a public with an eye to gasoline more than environmental costs, this catastrophe left us with an intense sense of betrayal.

That night as I sat down to supper with the blackened loon, I read the *Post-Intelligencer* report from Cordova, Washington's mental health center director: "People are feeling overwhelmed...and being frightened by their own tears," he said. In comparing the spill to the death of a child or spouse for fishermen, whose boats bobbed uselessly along Cordova docks, the director continued, "They can't believe they're crying. They're unaccustomed to a man breaking out in tears." A psychologist friend of mine told me her clients kept coming in with vivid dreams of the oil spill. "I've never seen a disaster go so deep," she said. "People are sobbing in their dreams."

Perhaps this first major spill in the far Northwest was the first to seep so profoundly into our collective consciousness. Now we must meet it—and all of the other environmental disasters that have since followed—face-to-face. It is right, of course, to deal with the oil spill, and all other forms of pollution as political, business, and environmental issues. We must assign responsibility if no one will step forward and accept it. With the

Valdez, we began with a captain known to have alcohol problems at the helm of such a potentially hazardous tanker. There is a terrible symmetry to a man polluted by alcohol commanding a tanker that pollutes so beautiful a body of water.

Then there is the underside of American big business. It is small comfort (and even smaller-minded corporate ethics) to discover that Exxon's farsighted insurance and liabilities are such that the company easily weathered any financial loss. Exxon absorbed so little, while it left the sea to absorb so much. And more than a decade after the Exxon *Valdez* spill, there is still evidence of damage done. It lingers in the sea bottom's sediment.

After my last supper with the loon, I stood on my backyard beach in the evening light, calling the gulls. I fed them leftovers from a friend's wedding. I didn't consciously connect those gulls who hung in midair cawing over the baked Brie, toast, and cookies with their Alaskan brethren until I realized with a jolt that I was surprised to see them still flying, white, not blackened by oil. As I gazed up at the flapping cloud of birds poised over me, I knew what was missing in all this oil spill response—no one was saying, "We're sorry" to the animals.

We humans depend on oil for much of our way of life. On a symbolic, collective level, these animals who have died are being devoured by our own hunger. We have not yet done our part in this predatory gift exchange. My father, who hunted and fed his family game all our childhood, taught us this: "You thank the animal for its sacrifice. It's like saying grace, except you also give thanks to the deer or elk because it lays down its life so you can keep living." Along with mourning these lost animals, we must also be grateful for their sacrifice in showing us this sad truth: We human animals are out of balance and out of control.

It is never too late to go quietly to our lakes, rivers, oceans, even our small streams, and say to the sea gulls, the great blue herons, the bald eagles, the salmon, that we are sorry. Sorry for the *Valdez* spill; sorry for the PCBs that run thick in our waters; sorry for the hundreds of individual spills by human residents; sorry for the singular piece of trash tossed onto their watery landscape.

And perhaps some of us can do something more: we will change our hearts. Only by changing our relationship with nature and her animals can we begin to accept responsibility and heal the savagery with which we have preyed upon the world, the mindset that author Daniel Quinn calls "a culture of maximum harm." This oil spill is, after all, a logical end of a mandate we have tacitly given our businesses: Do whatever you must to maintain our way of life.

What if, at our own private funerals for the animals, our partaking consciously in the animal and human gift exchange, we also changed our mandate to say that our survival *depends* upon all other forms of life? And what if each one of us proposed to give up just one act of personal pollution? Such rituals of mourning, gift exchange, personal responsibility, and individual action, might then begin to heal the spills.

In a Canadian book, *Renewal* (Theytus Books), a Cherokee woman, Gua Gua La (Barbara Elene Smith), tells an old tale of a time when the peoples of the sea and land were one. In our arrogance and isolation we have believed ourselves alone. We often see ourselves so separate that we have claimed dominion over all.

But the sea is not beneath us. It is our first womb, where we came from and now where we must, in our hearts, return if we are to establish a balance between land and sea. Gua Gua La's sea people's song to their land family served as my funeral song when the *Valdez* spilled. And every spill since then.

> Oh my Brother, What has happened?
> Once we were as one...
> But now you have changed
> You walk alone in the darkness of your own creation.
> You do not hear me when I call you
> My heart is sad. I weep for you my Brother
> And I sing of you in my prayers....

Whatever we land dwellers can do in our private eulogies, our promises, and water ceremonies, might bring some balance. Our small memorials will not assign blame or forgiveness. They can simply say to our fellow sea creatures that we are sorry; we are grateful for the gift; we see the sacrifice. And we will hold ourselves fast to learning this lesson that has cost them their lives.

Salmon People

We are Salmon People who are losing our salmon—and so we are losing ourselves. Only a hundred years ago, Native tribes such as the Muckleshoot who lived alongside the Green River told stories of walking across a lush stream, balancing on the backs of stalwart salmon. Thousands of salmon teeming, leaping, returning home with a single-mind, past predators of bear, bald eagle, sea lion, and fishers, upriver and down steep waterfall, following the precious scent of that first freshwater where they were born and will die, spawning.

Now we must fathom a Northwest in which salmon are so dwindled that for the first time in our history, we face a "zero option" on salmon fishing in Oregon, Washington, and along the British Columbia coast. And some of our legendary salmon and steelhead runs are now officially listed as endangered.

Tribal leaders, state and government fisheries managers, biologists, anglers, power companies, and ecologists are all seeking some solution to this salmon crisis that we have seen coming for a long time.

As early as autumn 1991 in *The Amicus Journal*, an article on a series of regional, voluntary "salmon summits" quoted Bill Bakke, executive director of Oregon Trout, as a "lone voice trying to bring attention to the plight of the salmon" for over two decades. Each group attending the salmon summits lobbied for their own interests, but the bottom line was only the economic benefit of salmon in our region. Bakke commented bleakly, "We're not going to have salmon here in the future, just like we don't have them on the East Coast."

Another salmon summit attendee, Ted Strong, Yakima Indian and executive director of the Columbia Inter-Tribal Fish Commission, noted the unwillingness of Northwesterners to "irreparably damage their well-being, their lives, to save salmon." He added, "We haven't had one salmon summit where the discussion was 'Let's discuss the cultural and spiritual values of salmon.'"

Our salmon are not simply a great main dish; they are not just an income producer or sporting event. Salmon are an indicator species for our homeland's health. If salmon are dying out, then literally a part of us is dying, too. Saving salmon is not just about fishing rights, habitat restoration, or breaching dams. It is also about connecting the fate of salmon to our own human destiny.

In Chief Sealth's words: "All things are connected." In this complex web of living species of which we are simply part, our scientific model of hierarchies and predators must give way to a holistic understanding of our interdependence.

Oweekeno First Nation, located about 250 miles north of Vancouver Island, British Columbia, is a microcosmos of what happens when the ecological balance is disrupted. In this remote tribal village of some eighty Oweekeno, Chief Sealth's words are tragically illustrated. For thousands of years the bear, human, and bald eagle populations lived together in harmony, fishing the Oweekeno Lake, the Wanuk River and some seventeen other rivers that flow into the region. Millions of salmon flourished and so the other species thrived. But in the 1990s all of this began to change. By 1999 the salmon run dropped to only 3,500 sockeye, a number many scientists calculate as close to extinction. Scientists describe Oweekeno as an "ecological and biological disaster." The culprits are many; over-fishing, logging, destruction of the salmon habitat, and a warming ocean.

This dramatic drop in salmon population, combined with the destruction of vast stretches of salmonberry, elderberries and blackberries by logging companies spraying with herbicides resulted in starving bears. Hungry Grizzly Bears and Black Bears, turned to Oweekeno village for sustenance, clawing at homes and raiding human territory. For months, the villagers tried to scare or lure the bears back into the wilderness. But in the end they were forced to kill several bears, an animal that is cherished in the Oweekeno stories, art, and religion.

The Oweekeno have also witnessed a dramatic decline of the bald eagle, another revered animal in the tribe's culture.

Bald eagles once flocked to the area by the hundreds when the salmon returned, but now there is only a handful. Oweekeno elder, Frank Hanuse, told *The Seattle Times* in an interview, "It's a sad day when the only eagles you see are at the dump."

The disruption of an ecological system, or what Chief Sealth first described as the web of life, results in the intricate interconnectedness of the environment collapsing into a hierarchy. Two species—in this case the bear and the human—struggle against one another for survival.

Echoing the wisdom of Chief Sealth, physicist and philosopher Fritjof Capra describes in his book, *The Web of Life: A New Scientific Understanding of Living Systems*, a paradigm that he calls "deep ecology." He explains: "It sees the world not as a collection of isolated objects, but as a network of phenomena that are fundamentally interconnected and inter-dependent. Deep ecology recognizes the intrinsic value of all living beings and views humans as just one particular strand in the web of life." Oweekeno as a microcosmos points to the rippling damage that happens in the larger world when we deny our interconnectedness.

Faced with the shadow of officially listed endangered runs, we must talk about just *who* the Salmon People are and why we need them. Native myths of the Pacific Northwest Coast teach us that there is a tribe of underwater peoples living in unseen symmetry with us land dwellers. There is a balance between land and sea, which must be honored. To keep this equipoise, certain land people would volunteer to exchange places with the salmon kin every fishing season, thus assuring the survival of both human and non-human.

Within this web of life there was not the hierarchy of food chain and top predators, which is what we learned in Earth Science courses. There was only the cycle of birth and death intermingled. The salmon teach us this every time they die; for in death, their bodies—desiccated from the heroic last swim home—spawn the next generation. If the salmon are not completing their great circle of regeneration, doesn't it have meaning for our children, our next born?

In the same week that zero options for salmon fishing were announced, *Newsweek* ran an article on the startling statistics that human male sperm counts are down 50 percent from 1938. The discovery began when an alligator hunter in Florida noticed that male alligators were only one quarter their normal size, their testosterone levels so low they were probably sterile. This led to further investigation of other species, including human male sperm counts. Additional research revealed that the pollutant PCBs in food and water had a molecular structure like estrogen. When a human infant nurses on mother's milk, the PCB pollutants enter the baby's blood and might cause everything from testicular malformation and undersized penises to eventual cancers, such as breast and testicular.

Along with this shocking news for us land dwellers breeding new generations, research studies of our mammal kin in the seas show that whale populations in the wild already have a 50 percent death rate among newborn calves. When the mother purges her blubber of all the heavy metals, toxic PCBs, and other ocean pollutants, the newborn's liver cannot process such poisons and the calf dies even as he suckles, seeking life.

Reductions of 50 percent in human sperm count, 50 percent survival rate of newborn whales, and near extinction of salmon are all interconnected. The link is the pollution in our waters, and our creation and consumption of hazardous materials—from plastics to hydroelectric dams—without thought to other species or our own natural habitat. Humans have behaved as if we were the only species who matters, as if our needs are more important than the ecosystem upon which we depend for survival. Is it any surprise that we now find our own mothers' milk polluted and our father's sperm count as diminished as those few salmon left to spawn?

How do we create and restore balance? How do we change this story so that in the future there will not only be stories to tell, but many children to listen? We can begin by remembering the truth of those old Native myths: That our fate is directly dependent upon every other species, from slug to salmon. As William Blake wrote, "Everything that lives is holy" whether it swims, flies, or walks.

When we use less electricity, we help more salmon leap up those devastating dams. When we take down those dams, we again share our rivers with the salmon. When we use less paper, we help preserve forest habitat and wetlands, which feed and nurture streams that feed the rivers. When we join environmental organizations, we contribute to clean-ups and legislation. When we recycle and buy fewer plastics, we stop the flow of PCBs into landfills and runoffs. If we identify ourselves with the salmon, our symbol, we may survive together.

In Alaska, there is legislation to protect the salmon and local fishing companies have voluntarily organized and formed the Alaska Trollers Association. Every spring, salmon counts are conducted on all the major Alaskan rivers to ensure the salmon population is plentiful year after year. If the count is low, fishing is reduced or terminated and the salmon continue upstream. When the salmon are at sea, the local commercial fishing companies fish from trollers, vessels that fish with lines and rods, and catch salmon individually. In contrast, trawlers greedily scrape the sea bottom for all life, scoop up everything, pulverize the salmon and anything else that gets in the way, and then dump and leave to die the unwanted portion of its haul. (Trawlers aided in the decimation of the cod population in the Northeast).

If we recognize ourselves as a part of the web of life, how do we participate in change? One simple option is to stop eating salmon. For those of us eating wild salmon from endangered areas such as Oregon, Washington, and British Columbia, we are, in effect, eating our own souls. Urban consumers can support the saving not the taking of salmon, much like the Oweekena tribe who recently have decided to forgo sustenance fishing in their homeland for now in order to support the salmon.

If we choose to eat salmon, let's support those in the industry who understand that longevity in the fishing business depends upon a commitment to the salmon. Alaskan fishers support and respect the animal from which they profit. If we eat salmon, eat wild Alaskan salmon.

Perhaps we can create a new mythology for the Salmon People of our times. Imagine that in another one hundred years our grandchildren will tell this story:

> Long ago when the salmon no longer offered us their gleaming backs to walk across the streams, when the land people forgot their bond with the underwater tribes and took so much we lost our balance, the land tribes gathered together. And they said, "We will not eat salmon again until the balance has been restored, until we see those shining backs filling every stream and sound."
>
> And because those human ancestors did not take their underwater brothers and sisters until the salmon returned in multitudes; and because our ancestors waited until their waterways were restored before feasting on salmon again—we, their great grandchildren, are surviving along with the salmon. We are still spawning together; we are still Salmon People.

River Tao

Water is the blood of the Earth, and flows
through its muscles and veins.... It comes forth in
metal and stone, and is concentrated in living creatures.
Therefore it is said that water is something spiritual.
　—Kuan Tzu

Every time I close my eyes, I return to drift down the Colorado River along its secret, swirling eddies and rock along its red, roiling rapids. Like destiny, this knowing river carves canyons, insists itself through bright granite, black-hard lava flow, and stone shale so old radiocarbon dating is useless to determine its age.

Never in my life, except for my first five years raised on a Forest Service ranger station in the High Sierras, have I been so out of time, disconnected from daily communication with what we on the river simply called "up there." So deep were we in 1.7-billion-year-old rock that no cellular phone could signal satellites, no transistor radio could scale sheer stone except one night a river runner announced "Got a few seconds of radio news. Biggest crowds in Britain since V-E Day for Princess Di's funeral." We all murmured our softly detached sympathy. Then he added, "And Mother Teresa died, too."

In silence we looked at each other. The soaring roar of the river seemed an appropriate response to the loss of two beloved caretakers of the human world. But this world seemed so far away, as did most every personal attachment—from grief to glory. We were simply *on the river*, fallen into a watery trance accompanied by cicada plainchant, the melodic call of canyon wren, the dinosaur caw of startled great blue heron, and twice the stealthy blue speed of a peregrine falcon.

"Give it to the river," someone murmured whenever anybody chatted too much about personal life or problems. Our lives before this canyon seemed so distant. "Not insignificant," sighed an older woman facing a fatal illness who found the Grand Canyon a fine place to contemplate eternity. Smiling, she stretched out along the silver pontoons of our boat. "Meaningful, our own lives, sure... but well, we're *here* now."

"Paleozoic seas once here, too," our boatman Art said. We dubbed him Art-More-Than-Science for his rapids finesse. We joined him in companionable quiet, gazing up at million-year-old shellfish and plants fossilized like a hieroglyphic language in stone. Every day we descended deeper into geologic time, a non-human story of bright angel shale with its turquoise green, black, and coral strata like woven patterns in a Navajo blanket.

We beheld billion-year-old jet-black Vishnu schist and pale crimson-purple Zoroaster granite, volcanic craters, and Native petroglyphs. One hematite-scrawled petroglyph showed a scorpion and big horn sheep, mother and child stick figures, a blazing sun—signs of a civilization more ancient even than the Hopi Indians who believe this Grand Canyon and river are their sacred *sipapu*, or naval of the universe.

At this swirling center where the Little Colorado runs into its namesake, we surfed a small rapid, our life jackets around our bottoms like diapers as the river carried us past boulders and holes. Muddy water streaming off our chilled bodies, we rose up like primeval Creatures of the Red Lagoon, birthed and baptized by river blood.

After a few days, my mind was clear and uncluttered, my body focused on tucking to take the next mighty rapid. This river so completely captured my imagination that like one possessed, I saw myself as merely an imprint of rock and river— my streaked hair was striated, my skin cleansed and scoured with the red grit of sediment, my clothes changed chameleon-like into the desert camouflage of terracotta. Days blurred as we drifted, studying our waterproof guides with miles marking each rapid like a sacred text of the river.

But at last I no longer glanced at my map to identify "Specter" or "Hermit" rapids, to calculate the sheer drops or cite pioneers who'd made this trip a century before, paddling backward in wooden dories. I no longer needed to know where I was. I was on the river. My way and its way were the same. Some afternoons lying back on the pontoons I'd read the only book I brought with me—the *Tao Te Ching* in an adaptation by

Ursula LeGuin. The *Tao* has always been my spiritual guide. As I floated, studying these 2,500-year-old epiphanies, surrounded by more enduring stone, I understood why Lao Tzu claimed water as his spiritual teacher and water's way as the "Way of Heaven."

"True goodness is like water," Lao Tzu wrote. "Water's good for everything." In this Grand Canyon nothing lives without water. With its rich sediment the river nourishes all it touches. Within this river *tao* I felt its strength and goodness. I also felt something else that I didn't understand, something unsettling and wrong. Every day the river rose or fell as if with a tide. Living in Seattle on Puget Sound, I am used to orienting and stabilizing myself by the ebb and flow of an inland sea. All life is dependent upon this daily sea-change—an authentic and natural cycle of moon, waves, and tide. But in my own body, made up mostly of water, I recognized that what made this Colorado River rise and fall was not at all natural.

When I asked boatman Dave Spillman about the strange rhythm, he sighed. "Upriver the Glen Canyon Dam manipulates the flow of the Colorado to make hydropower for cities like Los Angeles, Phoenix, and Las Vegas. For three-and-a-half years the Bureau of Wreck the Nation poured concrete to block this river. That was 1963, and what do we have now? Glen Canyon flooded. But the natural, cleansing floods are gone. Water temperatures used to be warm as 85 degrees, now they've plunged down to 46 degrees so that native fish species are going extinct. Each water droplet is spoken for seventeen times over, all the way south until this great river is just a trickle into the Gulf of Mexico."

"All dams die out," a German woman said. "They're made to last fifty to one hundred and fifty years—a blip in geologic time." A scientist, she further explained that dams eventually fill up with so much sediment the river simply chokes on its unflushed silt. "The Grand Canyon has more dams on it than any other river in the world." She nodded towards my water-soaked *Tao Te Ching*. "And have you heard the Chinese are constructing the most powerful dam ever built? On the Yangtze River? That huge dam will flood the Three Gorges—ravines that are as famous in China as this Grand Canyon. I wonder, what would Lao Tzu say about his countrymen's ambition? The Chinese compare their dam to building the Great Wall. And, like we in the West used to, they see the dam as a monument to their own greatness." She finished sadly, "All for electricity. All for power."

The next day finding land, shade, and solitude in the moist mist off Deer Falls, I read Lao Tzu's words: "Power is goodness.... Power is trust." Power, he seems to say, has little to do with worldly achievement or ambition. I wondered about our human needs, both for worldly power and electricity. Long before the discovery of man-made electricity, Lao Tzu knew that water equals power. He also knew that worldly power and control were illusions. He could not have known that centuries later we would dam up rivers, creating artificial power to run our daily lives. What happens to power when we mistake it for our own and don't honor the water source from which it is borrowed? What within us is illuminated, when we only light up a room, a city, a night desert—and not our own souls?

Lao Tzu says truly wise people are "the light that does not shine." There is nothing artificial or falsely bright about true power, just as there is a world of difference between Las Vegas neon and starlight. The river reminds us that water is the Way, not anything as recent as human evolution. When we interfere and change the rightful flow of rivers, we spiritually violate the Earth's own body and blood, as well as our own. For we are made of water and clay; our bodies first formed afloat in water's womb and buried in earth's.

At Deer Creek Falls, I listened to the thunder of snowmelt gushing from hundreds of feet above the canyon into a luminous freefall. This cascading wave shook the ground and yet its flow fed hanging primeval ferns; rivulets fell so delicately that they didn't disturb a yellow butterfly clinging to the Crimson Monkeyflower that climbed up slick stone. Here was the wild, natural flow of water and its power was humbling. I also felt sadness and an unbearable sense of loss. The river was once warm, now it is cold. The river's natural cycle of floods no longer enrich the waters with enough nutrients such as calcium, phosphorous, and bicarbonate that in turn nourish native plants and animals. We are now shaping this Colorado that for millions of years has shaped worlds of rock and river—and we don't really know what we are doing or the long-term consequences of all our river changes.

The boatmen talked about the artificial flood of April 1996 in which the dam was opened up for a "spike flow"—a scientific experiment to mimic nature's rejuvenating floods. Much was learned and there were many benefits from the artificial flood. More periodic floods may be needed in the future to support the river. But there are still so many questions about how to honor the river itself and assure the health of the canyon ecosystem.

While we have claimed the river for our own, we do not have water's wisdom or way of knowing what is best for the river. Though we control the Colorado and have made it the hardest working river in the world, we have not yet controlled ourselves enough to restore a fraction of what we've taken. So the Colorado that gives life to the West is itself seriously depleted. Even our river rafting trip, I realized, was owed to those who control the river. What would I give back? I wondered.

"You were asking about the dam," someone startled me from my reverie. "People are talking now about draining Lake Powell and restoring the Colorado River. Did you hear what that Sierra Club guy said? 'I don't want to be known as part of the generation that killed the Grand Canyon.'"

I agreed. "In my home, they've just voted to tear down the Elwha Dam and restore the river and its native salmon runs."

"There's some hope," she said.

I lay back, letting the waterfall thunder through my body. "Well," I sighed and stared up at the true power and greatness of this wild, world-changing water. Deer Creek Falls rocked the earth like a cradle. "Let's take the long view. Dams die out."

"So do rivers."

Sitting cross-legged a respectful distance from me, my river-running companion lay back and gazed up at the waterfall for a long time. Then she saw my waterlogged *Tao Te Ching* and closed her eyes. "Read something old as rock," she asked.

Mist swirled around us as I found my favorite passage "Water and Stone." I read it both as praise and requiem, as devotion and what I hope is destiny.

> What's softest in the world
> rushes and runs
> over what's hardest in the world.

River running over stone, over dam, over millenniums. River running true—to its story, to itself. May we be true as this river so that one day it is free to rise and fall with its own mystery, its Water Way.

Common Ground

Keepers of the Whale

Under a mid-December deluge, we drove the dangerous switchbacks and slick curves that define the narrow passage to Neah Bay, ancestral home of the Makah Nation. Along the waterfront highway jagged monolithic stones stood like ancient sentries in the windswept surf. These sea stacks are engraved with thousand year old petroglyphs of round-faced humans gazing at, and surrounded by, great open-mouthed whales. In the Northwest Coast tradition of interchangeable human and animal beings, both whale and human are called The People.

Migrating gray whales pass through Neah Bay on their twice-yearly migration between arctic feeding grounds and birthing lagoons in Baja, Mexico. Some whales stop in Neah Bay and become resident whales, living in the Bay's calm waters. The shared history of the Makah and the gray whale goes back some two thousands years—with the whale offering both physical and spiritual sustenance.

That winter of 1996, my Native American traveling companion Linda Hogan and I were writing a series for *The Seattle Times* on the Makah Nation's request to resume their whaling rights after a voluntary moratorium of some seventy years. The Makah's request to resume whaling resulted in an alarming concern among environmentalists as well as controversy among tribal members.

We journeyed to meet a seventy-three year old Makah elder named Alberta Thompson who is opposed to her tribe's plans to return to their lost tradition of hunting the gray whales. This was the first time Alberta was granting an in-depth interview, which would make widely known a dispute that had long simmered within the Makah tribe. In such a charged and volatile atmosphere, Alberta was scared—and so was I.

As novelists and nature writers, Linda Hogan and I had long worked on environmental issues. We were answering a request by several Makah elders who wanted to be interviewed. Linda had been a member of a Native Working Group of indigenous people on the reauthorization of the Endangered Species Act. I have written about cetaceans for two decades. In 1996 neither of us imagined the complexities of the five-year journey that would unfold regarding the Makah and their return to hunting.

As we drove down the main street of the Makah reservation, past the tribe's world-class museum, the marina under construction, and the Makah Maiden Cafe looking for Alberta's trailer, we had an uneasy inkling of what lay ahead.

The dark driving rain and low-hung fog lent a sense of foreboding to the reservation. And while at first glance Alberta Thompson was a genial grandmother, she was also formidable and stalwart. Her jet-black hair illumined by one startling silver streak runs back from her widow's peak like a lightning bolt. Alberta's somber tone and her dignified presence says she is very mindful of what she is about to do. In our interview, she meant to dispel the media's simplistic portrait of a battle brewing between conservationists and whale-hunting Indians on the high seas. She wanted to talk about her tribe's divisiveness on the issue of resurrecting a Makah whale hunt

"Most of the elders are against this hunt," Alberta began, sitting in a rocking chair. Her modest trailer was decorated with Makah carvings, hand-knit afghans, and walls crowded with photos of what Alberta describes as her "United Nationsof a family," in all human colors and all devoted to her. Family and friends call her Binki and by the stream of visitors, grandsons, and grown children, it was obvious that Alberta is much loved.

"I am speaking for the silent majority of Makah and the elders because they are afraid," Alberta began. "Some of the elders are so old they cannot stand up for hours at tribal meetings. Because they're against the hunt, the young men on the Tribal Council will not even give these old ones a chair to sit down." Alberta's vibrant voice trembled. "They are our elders, but the Tribal Council is not listening to them. The Tribal Council tells them that opposing the hunt will threaten our treaty rights." Alberta said firmly, "That is not true at all! Our treaty rights will stand, whether or not we go whaling."

Seven Makah elders, including the oldest living Makah, had signed a petition against the hunt, which Alberta and another Makah grandmother, Dotti Chamblin, presented at the International Whaling Commissions' (IWC) yearly meeting in June 1996 in Aberdeen, Scotland. Alberta grinned, "The Tribal Council told the IWC that I was 'dangerous.' I arrived in a wheelchair. What would make me, an old woman, so dangerous?"

In their passionate commitment to protect both the gray whales and the future reputation of the Makah and her grand-children, Alberta and Dotti were considered dangerous to the Tribal Council's goal of whale hunting. The anti-hunt petition by elders was simple and eloquent: "[We] think the word 'subsistence' is the wrong thing to say when our people haven't used or had whale meat-blubber since the early 1900s.... We believe the hunt is only for money."

At that time, the going rate internationally for one gray whale was estimated at $1 million. The Makah Tribal Council's most formidable allies against their own traditional elders was—and continues to be—the U.S. federal government. This rather unholy alliance between expedient, commercially minded tribal councils and federal forces united against older, more traditional tribal peoples has been and will continue to be a major issue of the twenty-first century environmental scene.

For an elder such as Alberta Thompson, the IWC meeting in Scotland was an unexpected, though short-lived success. At that 1996 meeting, the United States was persuaded to drop its request on behalf of the Makah the right to kill five whales a year.

Now, a couple of months later on a dreary, rain-drenched December day, Alberta's story rushed like a torrent as we struggled to take it down. For two days she talked. "If the Tribal Council had come to the elders and asked us about the old ways, the sacred traditions of the whale hunt," Alberta stressed, "if they had asked for and received the consent of the whole tribe, it would be different." Alberta noted that in the official tribal vote on whaling, only 104 of the 600 total Makah tribal members there actually cast a vote on the whaling proposal, with 70 tribal members voting in favor of the whale hunt. Many tribal members did not attend the meeting. "This was not a consensus," Alberta said. "Just a few hardliners on the Tribal Council pushed this whaling idea through and now they are threatening those of us who stand up against them."

Elder Dotti Chamblin joined us on the second day to add her story. Younger and more reserved with outsiders than Alberta, Dotti was equally committed to speaking out for the whale and other frightened Makah.

"It's grandmothers fighting this fight against them," Dotti said of the Makah Tribal Council. Dotti is a traditional healer and tribal social worker who ran for the Tribal Council in 1996 and lost to a pro-whaling member. Her great-grandfather, Ba-Ba-Sit, who died in 1907, was one of the last Makah to hunt whales. Dotti's family still knew some of the ancient whaling songs. Raised in the Old Way, Dotti feared for the future of her tribe as they cast about for lost traditions.

"The Tribal Council issued a memo that nobody was to talk to the newspaper," explained both. "They wanted to banish from the tribal rolls those of us from the reservation who oppose whaling. This fear of banishment really stopped a lot of people from helping us." If the Tribal Council banished them, it meant they might lose their tribal benefits, such as health care and some financial support.

Because the Makah are both members of a tribal nation, as well as citizens of the United States, they live in two worlds and sometimes these two sets of laws are at odds. The women hoped that young people and tribal elders would be allowed to talk openly about the ancient relationship of both spiritual tradition and physical subsistence between the Makah and the gray whales. Why, they wondered, was there no democratic atmosphere for open debate? "I am Makah and an American citizen," Alberta said. "Where are my First Amendment rights?"

If this were simply a story of an American citizen being censored, harassed, and threatened by the FBI or another federal government agency, it would be a page one story; the woman's case would be taken up by American Civil Liberties Union or some other watchdog, civil rights group. But because Alberta Thompson is a Native American and subject to tribal government laws, because the Makah Tribal Council can make unilateral decisions without consensus from tribal members, Alberta's dual-citizenship ironically gives her less freedom and recourse than the majority of U.S. citizens have.

When she approached lawyers who might represent her in a lawsuit against the Makah Tribal Council, even lawyers who specialized in Native rights turned down Alberta's case. They did not want to jeopardize their status or position as legal representatives of tribal councils throughout the country; many councils are involved in lawsuits against the government on gambling, environmental issues, and redress for a long history of U.S. government wrongdoing.

Alberta Thompson and other frightened elders were thus very vulnerable to the Makah Tribal Council's threats against her right to free speech. In addition, she is an elderly woman marginalized and often ignored by a media that has pitted the simplistic polarities of either saving whales *or* Indian culture. And the federal government was up to its eyeballs in international free-trade tactics using the Makah for its own ends—to keep economic peace and free trade with the whaling nations of Japan, Norway, and Russia.

Japan and Norway—two nations that continue to defy a worldwide whaling moratorium—had been advising the Makah Tribal Council on hunting whales. Conservationists worldwide were worried that the Makah whale hunt would set a dangerous precedent that would open the door for a global resumption of whaling. Resumption not on the basis of nutritional needs, such as the Eskimo's nutritional subsistence on bowhead whales, but on a "cultural need." This Makah precedent would then justify Japanese, Norwegian, and other Native American coastal tribes to hunt whales, not by proving a direct, subsistence dependence, but by a more elusive and historical claim of restoring a lost tradition. And if this "cultural whaling" soon led to commercial whaling, who would be able to stop a new century of renewed, world-wide whaling?

Most of the world believes that after decades of international whaling moratoriums, the great whales of the world are "saved." This is scientifically untrue; many whales, such as bowheads and right whales are on the brink of extinction. However, the gray whale has been recently removed from the endangered species list, though many scientists still dispute the extent of the gray whale's recovery. Very little in the media informs people that there is also worldwide, pirate whaling going on as well as commercial whaling by Russia, Norway, and Japan under the guise of "research" and in flagrant violation of the IWC moratoriums.

In the 1990s, pressures of politics, free trade, and globalization were hard at work to undermine the future of whales on this blue planet. According to *Mother Jones*, this new category of "cultural whaling" comes from the Office of Environmental Quality, under Vice President Al Gore. How ironic that this self-described "environmental" candidate for the presidency is credited with ushering in a new century of "cultural whaling".

In 1993, Vice President Al Gore met with Norwegian Prime Minister Gro Harlem Brundtland and secretly signaled to the Norwegians that the United States would not interfere with their plans to expand commercial whaling. Gore's infamous Norwegian memo was leaked to the press and published in full-page ads with the caption "Blood and Gore." In the memo, the Vice President repeated the United States commitment to stand by and not interfere with Norwegian attempts to overturn the IWC ban on commercial whaling. Gore wrote: "This strengthens my argument for a need for a scheme that will allow resumption." Gore hoped to keep free trade options open to Norway and Japan by not interfering with their commercial whaling.

The Makah fit right into this U.S. free trade zeal that superceded any environmental issues or concern for the tribe's own welfare. Just as the Makah had been devastated a century ago by a federal government bent on conquest, acquisition, and destruction of the Native peoples, so now they were being used in a cynical international game with commerce, not culture, as the real bottom line.

The U.S. Commerce Department funded the Makah to set up their own Whaling Commission with a grant of $310,000, some of which was used for travel to Japan. The irony was not lost on many conservationists. This would be a federally funded hunt in an officially designated marine sanctuary by a small tribe (1,800 enrolled members) whose reservation is seized with massive unemployment, substance abuse, and tribal government corruption. The isolated Makah would be the pawn for an international resumption of commercial whaling. But what would the Makah get? The blame, shame, and worldwide condemnation, as well as the feared backlash of racism.

Makah elders such as Alberta Thompson dreaded that this backlash would ripple down through future generations. She worried how repercussions might do extensive damage to her grandchildren's spirits in much the same way that smallpox had devastated Makah ancestors' physical health a century ago. This inner struggle among the Makah had been kept secret, confined to their tribal land. A few families had seized power on the Makah Tribal Council; and their harassment of anti-whaling Makah tribal members was sanctioned by the federal government. By choosing to back the bullies, the U.S. government continued its history of supporting puppets and dictators—as it had in Nicaragua, El Salvador, and Guatemala among others. By disallowing the right to free speech, by threatening anti-whaling Makah with banishment from tribal rolls, by discouraging an open dialogue on the whaling issue, the Makah Tribal Council was operating a corrupt government with full sponsorship of the United States. And yet through all the inner dissent, the U.S. federal government portrayed itself as a champion of Native American treaty rights, implying that the government was at last righting an historic wrong. Actually, they were perpetuating the manipulation and abuse of tribal peoples, fragmenting them from within.

Yet as much as the Makah were pawns of the federal government, their own tribal government and their past also enslaved them. In fact, the Makah Nation, like the United States, has a dark history of slavery. The ancient Makah had a patriarchal, hierarchical society that also included a slave culture among its own people. To this date, some Makah view any descendant of a Makah slave as an inferior, or their version of an "untouchable." In an act of inner-tribal classism, one of the most hurtful and untrue epithets hurled at Alberta when she first opposed the whale hunt was that she was just a slave, directly descended from the ancient Makah slave class. In other words, what she had to say was not of importance because of her ancestry.

As we ended our second long day of interviewing, Dotti Chamblin talked more about the history of environmental and tribal government corruption. "There's something very wrong here," she said. "We created a stir just by seeking the truth and asking them [the Tribal Council] to tell it. Because of our treatment, no one else will speak up for the rest of the people.... The Tribal Council ostracized us. They treat me badly. It's difficult to get health care. It's not the Makah way." She paused, then added that there is a young, Western faction that is in breach of tradition.

"No one in this village has a direct relationship with the whale any longer," Dotti Chamblin finished wearily. She and Alberta did not want death to be the only link between the Makah and their ancient spiritual ally, the gray whale. Before contact, the Makah lived for two thousand years with the gray whale as their spiritual and physical mainstay. The gray and humpback whales were food, oil, inspiration for art, and sacred, often secret, Makah traditions. In those days, the Makah hunters were from the most elite families; their training was rigorous and the survival of the tribe depended upon the hunters' skills. But that whaling tradition was voluntarily stopped by Makah elders early in the twentieth century when the Yankee whaling ships had slaughtered so many gray whales they swam on the brink of extinction. And for the past seventy years, the Makah have voluntarily stopped their whale hunt.

Alberta Thompson leaned forward in her rocking chair and her wide, generous face was set in a stoic expression. The Makah no longer need the gray whale to subsist, she said. "It is a different time. It is a different ocean, and a different whale. If the Makah go whaling," she predicted, "then some of us Makah will be out on the boats to try to protect the whales from slaughter."

Alberta concluded our conversation by ruminating over potential injury to the whaling crew. "I asked Ben Johnson, the chairman of the Makah Whaling Commission, 'Who is going to be responsible for the first deaths?'" explained Alberta. "Because there will be deaths."

Two years later during the spring 1999 Makah whale hunt, Alberta Thompson was indeed there on the marina dock among the protesters who wanted to protect the gray whales from her tribe's hunters. She would suffer much for her beliefs. And most often in the media glare, Alberta would stand alone, representing the other Makah elders who had been silenced by the Tribal Council.

Within a year of the IWC meeting in Scotland, the federal government and the Makah Tribal Council regrouped and in October 1997 told the world they had succeeded in their quest to return to whaling for the first time in almost a century off American shores. Through a back-door negotiation at the IWC, the U.S. government brokered a deal with Russia to grant five whales per year from the Russian whale-killing quota to the Makah. This means a quota of twenty whales killed or thirty-three wounded, whichever comes first, over a period of five years. Against fierce dissent from over twelve IWC nations, such as Australia and Britain, the U.S. federal goverment and the Makah Tribal Council announced that they had been granted the right to go whaling. "We won," they said, as if it were a war. But the United States/Makah claim is still internationally disputed.

As the battle intensified, the Makah reservation was a troubled place, full of dissent that the Tribal Council tried to cover up. Alberta was again ordered by the council not to talk to outsiders or give interviews to the press. These orders she ignored, but other elders were more fearful. How many of the elders could stand against the full power of their Tribal Council and the U.S. government? And over the next year every other elder would fall silent as they watched Alberta alone take on the fury of their Tribal Council.

While she was oppressed on the reservation, Alberta

found dignity and respect among international audiences. She was invited to speak in Australia as an honored guest at a worldwide gathering of indigenous elders. Together with her family member, Amelia Davisson, Alberta journeyed to Baja, Mexico on a Jean-Michel Cousteau expedition to witness the gray whales in their warm birthing lagoons.

Up and down the West Coast, from Canada to Baja, there is a thriving whale watching business that brings in millions of dollars to local, coastal peoples. Davisson and other moderate Makah explored a long-term prospect to stimulate the Makah's depressed economy by watching, not killing whales. She wondered if this would be a way for future generations to engage with the Makah spiritual heritage and connection with the gray whales.

"This would be a wonderful thing to leave our children," Davisson hoped.

There were fragile, behind-the-scenes negotiations between conservationists and moderate Makah who were looking for alternatives to the whale hunt. In the summer of 1997, a modest whale watch was organized to take a new generation of Makah to the ocean, including Jerry Lucas, a moderate, undecided member of the Makah Tribal Council. Jerry was intrigued by the economic prospects of a whale watching venture in Neah Bay. In the midst of a fierce, inter-tribal conflict over the looming whale hunt, a small group of Makah ventured into ancestral waters to observe the whales. Many of the Makah had never even seen a whale up close.

In a windswept coastal rain, what Jerry Lucas and Alberta Thompson teasingly called the Makah's "liquid sunshine," they climbed aboard the 54-foot boat *Discovery* docked at the spacious new Neah Bay marina. They were joined by Alberta's daughter, Tracy, three of Alberta's young grandsons, one adult grandson's wife, Amelia Davisson, a naturalist and gray whale expert, John Calambokidis, Stan Butler of Whales Alive, Toni Frohoff Ph.D., a marine mammal biologist and consultant to The Humane Society of the United States (HSUS), Will Anderson of Progressive Animal Welfare Society (PAWS), and myself. We hoped to encounter resident whales who consider Neah Bay their summer home.

In her yellow slicker with a gray-wool scarf tied under her chin, Alberta excitedly scanned the misting horizon for signs of a gray whale. "We see whales from shore," she said, "but this is the first time in my life I'll see whales from out on my Native waters." Alberta Thompson had not been out into Neah Bay since her childhood in the 1920s.

As the rainstorm eased and the swells ebbed, our naturalist pointed to the north near huge, flat-topped rocks encircled by seagulls. "Earlier today we saw a whale over by those rocks. Let's take another look."

The boat tipped as everyone ran to one side to raise their binoculars and try to be the first to spot the misting blow of a surfacing gray. Around us, the pristine, mysterious shores of Neah Bay took on a shine in the wavering sunlight. Jerry stretched his arms wide and called out over the engine, "I want you to see what Makah take for granted! Can you believe all this beauty?"

Luminous waves with rolling white caps stretched beyond sight. Eagles, gulls, and cormorants soared above us. Sleeping sea lions and diving osprey adorned the stony beaches and close to shore rose the famous Seal Rock and Sail Rock—those ancient monoliths with their whale and people petroglyphs, which I'd glimpsed on my first trip to Neah Bay. These rocks signaled this seafaring people that home was in sight. Today they held out the hope of greeting another seafaring species, the great gray whale.

"All this has been a part of our Makah culture for thousands of years," Jerry observed as he surveyed the Makah's coastal homeland.

On the bow of the boat, Alberta was surrounded by her grandsons all sharing one set of binoculars. The boys were thrilled at the prospect of encountering a whale.

"I wish I had the eyes of an eagle," one of Alberta's grandsons sighed, passing the binoculars to his cousin.

"Thunderbird," this cousin corrected. "That's what we call them... the thunderbird is our Makah tribe's symbol." After a moment's thought, he added, "The whale, too... that's a big deal for the Makah." He stopped, shook his head as if confused. "Some people want to hunt them. Other people, like my Grandma, don't."

"I just want to see one real close!" interrupted his cousin. "I want to touch a whale like Grandma." The boy beamed, his slicker soaked, his baseball cap and his dark curls damp. We were all drenched from the morning rainstorm, but excitement kept us out on the bow of the boat hoping for a glimpse of a whale. "Grandma touched a mama whale down in Mexico!"

Alberta smiled and leaned against the railing as our boat rose and fell in the waves. "Yes, I told them," she laughed. "I'll tell that story for the rest of my life. The gray whale mothers and calves came up so close to our boats. They trusted us and wanted to make physical contact. Can you imagine that?"

As we rocked back and forth on our sea legs, eyes set on the horizon, Alberta talked on about her winter trip to Baja, Mexico to the birthing lagoons of the great grays. "Oh my," she began softly and her grandsons leaned against her as they listened. "That mother or grandmother whale just rose up out of those warm waters right under my hand. She wanted to be stroked and scratched—all those barnacles, you know. She looked me straight in the eye—mother to mother—and I burst into tears when I saw she had a little one with her, a baby calf. She was showing me her calf and asking me to take care of it when they made their big swim back up past Makah and on up to Alaska. She was saying, 'Look after us. It's a hard journey and some of us won't make it.'"

"We've come full circle. The whales we see today may be the whales we touched down in Baja," smiled Amelia Davisson.

Amelia had researched whale watching and discovered that throughout the world—from New Zealand to British Columbia—whale watching had transformed depressed economies into flourishing whale watching meccas. Indigenous peoples in such places as Manila had received government and corporate grants to sponsor whale watching businesses. In Washington State alone, it had become a multi-million-dollar business. All this promised Amelia and others in the Makah community that whale watching might be a viable option for the tribe.

"We want to stay in Neah Bay," Amelia declared as the boat edged closer to Seal Rock. She was mid-term in her pregnancy with her second child, whom she hoped to raise on the reservation, proud of his Makah heritage.

"We want to stay here with our families. It's so beautiful and this whale watching would be a wonderful thing to leave our children."

As our boat rose up to meet gusts of wind and wave, one of those boys suddenly yelled out, "Over there! Look!"

Once again the boat tipped to one side as everyone rushed to see tail flukes slap the water like a greeting. All at once, several huge whales breached and dove around us in four directions. We were surprised at how easily the whales accepted our presence, and the naturalist explained, "These whales haven't been hunted here for many decades."

"Call the whales, Grandma," one of her grandsons implored as if Alberta had secret powers with the great grays. She closed her eyes, and we all grew silent as if fully expecting that she did. We rose and fell with the boat, then a grandson whispered, "What's that? It's... it's... oh, wow!"

A sleek gray-and-white belly streaked underwater right toward us in the bow of the boat. Fast, silver-gray and massive, the whale slid alongside our boat. We all held our breath. Five feet from the boat, the great gray surfaced with a mighty glide upwards so its barnacled back was next to our handrails. As the whale rose, she slightly turned her huge dark eye, fully exposed as if to get a good look at these gape-mouthed humans. We exhaled in an explosion of shouts and high-pitched screams. We were not afraid of the whale's size and nearness, but rather absolutely exhilarated.

"He looked at me!" one of the boys shouted. "Right at me!"

"She's got a really big eye!" another added. "She saw all of us."

"I wonder if she recognized us?" Alberta asked softly, then shook her head in wonder. "Thank you," she called after the whale. "Oh, thank you."

We all felt grateful to this whale who had raised up a huge head and curiously taken us in. Yet I wondered if the whale needed to be more wary. After decades of protecting the gray whale, many whales are known as Friendlies because they initiate contact with humans, particularly in Baja lagoons. Humans taught the whales that they could trust us. The prospect of these same whales being hunted off U.S. coasts is heartbreaking.

"That mother whale in Baja," Alberta said, "had a huge harpoon scar on her side. That means some human tried to kill her probably in Alaska where they still go whaling. And yet..." Alberta paused to wipe away her tears. "And yet that mother whale still showed me her calf... even though she knew my kind had tried to kill her once. Do you understand that? I don't. I just know that I have to honor it. And to teach my children and children's children to honor this creature who can forgive us the way God talks about forgiveness."

We all stood still in our bright-yellow slickers. There was a sense of all being well between the whales and us. As if to underscore our contentment, the sun gleamed through gray clouds and within minutes we were peeling off our slickers and rain hats, surrendering to light and warmth.

"You see," the naturalist said, "we didn't have to go very far to see resident whales. That's because the waters off Neah Bay are calm and protected."

Our naturalist further explained to us that these shallow and quieter waters provide even better whale watching opportunities, not only because of their protection, but because there are many resident whales here.

Biologist Toni Frohoff added, "Most whale watching operations only operate during the migration months until late spring." Pausing to photograph a nearby whale as it breached off our bow, she continued, "Whale watching here might even be better than other areas along the West Coast. That's because in Neah Bay the resident gray whales offer up to nine months a year for possible encounters." The highest rate of tourism in Washington State occurs mid-to-late summer when most coastal whale watching operations are already closed for the season. Neah Bay whale watching would fill a void and meet the needs of many tourists who equate seeing whales with seeing Washington.

"We are hoping the public will recognize that our relationship with whales has evolved," said Will Anderson of PAWS, who has been a longtime friend of Alberta's and worked with other Native peoples who oppose the hunt. "After we stopped killing whales, many of us, Native and non-Native, developed strong environmental, even spiritual bonds with this other species."

"If the Makah ever decide to do whale watching," predicted Stan Butler of Whales Alive, "so many people will come to their program that it will be an instant success." Butler directed his comments to Jerry Lucas as a member of the Tribal Council. "No one knows this land and these waters like the Makah. You have a cultural history with the whale that would give your whale watching more dimension than just a business venture. Because Makah tribal history is intertwined with the natural history of the gray whale, who better to tell this interdependent story of First Peoples and whales?"

The Makah Cultural and Research Center, an internationally-known museum of tribal heritage, describes the Makah whalers as once being high-ranking leaders who "devoted their whole lives to spiritual readiness" for hunting the great whales. The Makah sacred songs, whaling gear, and family ceremonies go back thousands of years. Their bond with the whale was once both spiritual and for subsistence. But according to Alberta Thompson and Dotti Chamblin, few if any of today's Makah have ever tasted whale meat. The diet of many Makah, like others in this country who live below the poverty line, is low in nutrition, often consisting of fast food and pre-packaged fare. Diabetes afflicts much of the Native populations.

In addition, there are increasing scientific concerns about the safety and nutritional value of whale meat. In the arctic, Inuit women who subsist off a diet primarily of whale meat are now unable to breastfeed their children due to the toxicity of their breast milk. It is believed their milk has been contaminated by heavy amounts of PCBs in the ocean that finds its way into the whale's blubber.

As we watched the grays cruise amiably by our boat, we discussed among ourselves the big question: Would a return to whaling really restore the Makah's spiritual tradition with the whale—or would it instead threaten this ancient and intimate bond with a species still precarious?

Amelia Davisson smiled as she described the possibilities of combining bird watching, whale watching, and a boat visit to the Makah's sister village of Nitnaht across the Strait of Juan de Fuca on British Columbia's Vancouver Island. "We have so much of our culture to share. The Makah Canoe Club and Dance Troupe have gone as far away as Germany to share our traditions. There's camping here and fishing and so much history. Our carvers and artists are among the best in the world... if we can just get people up here to visit us and the whales."

"You know, I'd forgotten how beautiful my own home waters are," Jerry mused as he pointed out the jagged splendor of Slant Rock and Mushroom Rock. A tall, impressive Makah man in his mid-forties, Jerry was friendly and open during all our conversations. As we neared the familiar rocks where Jerry had often fished with his family, we were all delighted to spot so many sea otters feeding there. Long endangered, the sea otter is rarely seen anywhere in this country except around Neah Bay and in Northern California. Jerry pointed to shore, "There's Warm House, our summer fishing village... where I almost drowned."

As Jerry fondly told the story of how his fishing galoshes almost drowned him when he was swept overboard, he gazed around at the majesty of his Makah homeland and he fell pensive. At last he said, "We want the opportunity to just stay and live in Neah Bay for another thousand years." Then Jerry's face lit up. "Can you just see it? Can you just see a whale watching boat full of Makah kids... a whole school bus of young Makah meeting the whales?" He began to share Amelia's vision for a return to the whales—but this time as watchers and keepers, not as hunters. Jerry would remain neutral on the issue of whaling, and his time on the Tribal Council ended before the whale hunt of May 1999.

As we floated together in the rare sunlight, surrounded by whales, there was a camaraderie and peacefulness, as if we had finally left far behind the divisive politics of the Makah whale hunt. We were united by the simple wonder and pleasure of Neah Bay. Drifting in serene waters, we all fell so quiet and content that no one was surprised when another young gray whale glided alongside us with a sudden, whooshing breath that misted over our heads like a blessing. Alberta and her three grandsons leaned way out over the deck with their arms outstretched to almost touch the gray whale lolling on her luminous back to greet these hopeful humans. Lingering surprisingly long with Alberta and her grandsons, the young gray gazed up at them with a benevolent, unblinking eye.

As I watched Alberta and her grandsons, I felt a rush of conflicting feelings—hope in my heart for a resolution and dread in my belly over an impending hunt. This emotional seasickness belied the calm waters on this particular bright summer day. There was no fear between people and whale, simply the bond, the abiding trust. Alberta and her grandsons seemed more a part of the Makah's future than the past. *But what about the present?* I wondered. *And what was to come?*

"Grandma, look!" called one of the boys. "I almost

touched that whale!"

Alberta and her grandson called out to the gray who floated near the boat, breathing steadily—inspirations and expirations of another mammal so mysterious and yet somehow so familiar to us. Fifty million years ago, these ancient grays also lived on land. Whale skeletons reveal vestigial hind limbs and long fingers like huge human hands inside their evolved pectoral fins. As land and sea mammals, we humans are related to the great whales, but they are our elders. And this ancient, interrelated mammalian lineage reminds us that long before there were humans or tribes, treaties or laws, there were whales.

Their Makah ancestors had never encountered this: a gray whale population almost lovingly hand-raised in Baja birthing lagoons, protected from hunting for half a century, and now so trusting they are also residents of Neah Bay. The gray whales had become an extended part of the Makah tribe and the life of all coastal peoples.

As the gray whale at last prepared to dive and leave us, we all leaned towards the whale, hands reaching, hoping to touch. The whale lazed nearby, rolling to look at us one last time. A dark eye the size of a softball, barnacles embedded in her huge silver-gray snout, the whale just kept looking at us as if memorizing these people so happy to meet her gaze. This was a gift exchange between humans and animals, a reunion and acknowledgment that we are all still The People.

The young gray dove so deep that we did not see her for about ten minutes. Again she surfaced, still companionably near our boat. Alberta took me aside and held my arm to steady herself on the gently rocking deck. "What if the tribe really does go whaling?" she asked. "What if the world sees and judges that? I just hope the world will know that some of us Makah tried to stop it."

Alberta knew that although the Makah are a very small, isolated tribe, they are not insulated from the world's glaring spotlight. Would history judge their tribe's return to whaling harshly? Would the Makah suffer from an international backlash? Would the harsh public scrutiny embitter and shame the Makah?

"In reservation school," Alberta confided, "some of the kids call my grandsons names because they love the whale as I've taught them. I don't want my grandsons to suffer as I do because I'm speaking out for the whale. But I also want them to know that the Makah and the gray whale have always belonged together." Alberta fell silent as the boys exulted in the gray who still stayed alongside our boat.

"This is not really about treaty rights," Alberta reminded us. "It's about the future stability of our people. My fear is that this whaling issue will divide and fragment our tribe. And that it will backlash against our children. What is their future with the whale?" Alberta asked softly.

The prestige and spiritual respect once given Makah whalers when their society was separate and intact would not be granted the next generation of Makah in today's world. Just as Alberta's family is a small United Nations, her grandsons are growing up in a global village. In the future, they must see themselves reflected in that wider world as well as in the traditions of their ancestors. As we circled slowly in synch with several curious whales, Alberta shook her head as she balanced against the rocking boat. There was a sense that she carried many others on her solid shoulders.

Alberta took off her glasses and closed her eyes, then she leaned towards me and asked in an uncharacteristically sad voice, "What if the hunters kill a Friendly?" Tears filled her eyes as she considered the posibility. "What will I tell my grandchildren?"

In silence, we stared at the next generation. Her grandsons were unaware of her sorrow and her scrutiny as they laughed and waved, calling out to another surfacing whale. "They are the future," Alberta said quietly, proudly. "But what will we all have to go through to finally get to their time with these whales? What will the whales go through until my grandsons can grow up and protect them?"

In the spring of 1999, about one mile offshore and in the open ocean close to the Point of Arches, just south of the Makah reservation, another gray whale glided right up to a boat to greet humans. They were not Makah elders or children. Instead the boat held young Makah hunters in their twenties and thirties who wielded harpoons and a .50-caliber antitank gun. Trusting, the juvenile whale turned on her side to better see the young men scrambling for their weapons, their support motorboat close behind. In a huge circle around this whale and hunting canoe was a Coast Guard boat patrolling the federal "no-entry zone" against a flotilla of smaller protest boats. One by one, the protest boats had been boarded and seized by the Coast Guard.

All that was left in this marine sanctuary was the Makah canoe and a young gray whale.

And for the first time in seventy years these dark blue waters ran bright red with the blood of a harpooned gray whale. Millions watched the kill live as the wounded whale tried to flee, pulling the Makah hunters a short distance, three harpoons lodged in her thirty-foot body. In a circle around the dying whale, the bloodied waters swelled outward in crimson waves to include the canoe. Three times the hunter shot the young gray, one bullet through the brain in a mortal explosion.

After several minutes of struggle the juvenile gray whale submerged—not of her own strength, for she was dead. Her open mouth taking in seawater she sank down and down. No one among the hunters had the equipment or the skill to dive into the water to sew up the baleen mouth of the gray, as their Makah ancestors would have. So the gray sank to the ocean floor where she would have stayed, resting like a shipwreck.

What should have been several hours and a triumphant tow to the nearby shore turned into an all-day ordeal. The Coast Guard had to assist the Makah by retrieving the sunken whale. Using an air pump, they inflated the dead whale enough to coax the carcass upward with an onboard wench. By early evening, the world watched the international news story of an exuberant whaling crew, with assistance from the Coast Guard support boat, tow the dead whale ashore.

Onshore someone jumped onto the back of the whale with a rattle and sang a song. Other young Makah men clambered atop the broad back of the gray whale and raised their fists in the air, exchanging triumphant high-fives. Some of the celebrants did back flips off the whale. News cameras rolled while some Makah claimed victory. Others in the tribe stood off in the distance, separate from the celebration, concerned and contemplative. Alberta was interviewed at home. Openly she wept. She hoped the whale's killing might make a difference in the future. "I couldn't look into its eyes and not feel anything," Alberta mourned.

In Seattle, I sat cross-legged in front of my television as the news played and replayed the whale kill. After the first live footage, the news reports never again showed the harpoon and .50-caliber shooting. I believe the media decided the bloody waters were too disturbing for viewers. Instead the news reports cut from the first throw of the harpoon to the mortally wounded whale towing the canoe, to the gray disappearing into the depths.

Helplessly, I placed a hand on the television screen as if to comfort the dying whale, as if to again take Alberta's arm and steady her as she stood weeping. Many of us called Alberta and other Makah that day; but at Alberta's there was only an answering machine.

After the television cameras had stopped rolling, the Makah went home, leaving no one to complete the ancient ceremony of singing all night to the sacrificed whale. That night a man the Makah had hired from the subsistence whale-hunting Inuit tribe patiently flensed the whale. He labored long into the night with little company except an official representative from National Marine Fisheries who had to oversee the whale hunt to be sure it was done within the rules agreed upon between Makah and the U.S. government. To many Makah this abandonment of sacred tradition seemed a grave dishonor to the spirit of the young gray. As one Makah elder said, "When the man kills the whale, the only part he takes is the saddle or the dorsal fin. He takes that to a smokehouse for four days. He meditates and prays. On the fourth day, the spirit of the whale leaves. Well, these kids took the dorsal fin and put it in the backyard and left it there. I couldn't believe it when I heard it...."

So that long, lonely night, the Inuit man butchered the whale, sawing through surprisingly thin layers of blubber. No one could know then that in the next few months during the 1999 spring northern migration, a record-high of one hundred gray whales would wash ashore, representing the estimated eight hundred who died at sea. The whales would be diagnosed as having starved to death. Scientists were puzzled and wondered if their deaths were due to lack of food or because of polluted waters.

After the May hunt, the backlash against the Makah was intense and immediate. Internationally there were harsh criticisms leveled against the Makah and the U.S. government. In the Northwest an outpouring of angry letters filled page after page of *The Seattle Times*. Again, the media portrayed only a polarized split between tribal peoples and environmentalists without giving much attention to the moderates on either side or to the protests from tribal peoples themselves against the hunt. The First Nations Environmental Network in Canada criticized the hunt and ran their protest on the Internet, "We are deeply concerned and saddened by the killing of a whale at Neah Bay.... At this point in human history, we feel that spiritually and morally, the act of killing whales cannot be justified."

The Quileute tribe on the Olympic Peninsula, neighbors to the Makah, had already announced they would not restore their own cultural tradition of whale hunting. Chris Morganroth, a Quileute carver and teacher, told the Olympic Peninsula newspaper, *Peninsula Daily News*, "We honor the whale in our songs, drumming and dancing." And Karsten Boysen, information and education director for the Quileute tribe, added, "Our Tribal Council passed a resolution in 1988 that we would not take any whales. This choice not to hunt gray whales still stands now that the whale has been delisted."

The inter-tribal struggle among the Makah after the whale hunt has spread across the waters, across the artificial boundaries of the United States and Canada. The Nuu-chah-nulth Tribal Council announced their plans to return to their lost tradition of whaling, but the more traditionally minded Nuu-chah-nulth tribal members are speaking out against the hunt.

The summer after the Makah's spring 1999 hunt, traditional Nuu-chah-nulth watched the 250 to 300 resident whales who have made their summer home off Vancouver Island for the past three decades mysteriously disappear, seriously affecting the usually prosperous whale watching industry for Canadian Native and non-Natives. The Nuu-chah-nulth spoke out against their U.S. cousins' controversial hunt.

Nuu-chah-nulth member Qaamina, his father, Stanley, and Sam Jr., a respected elder and member of the prestigious Canadian Science Committee, gave interviews to their country's newspapers, however their opinions were not widely reported in the U.S. media.

"My father told me, 'This was not a spiritual hunt,'" stated Qaamina of the Ahousaht First Nations. "This was not what it used to be. My father also told me this: 'To be a great hunter, you don't hunt the timid whale. It would be like shooting your own dog for supper.'"

Qaamina also said after the hunt, "I had a very dark feeling. We must treat animals the same way we want to be treated. Our gray whales and cedar forests are sacred." He concluded by saying that his father taught him the gray whales are intelligent and can communicate over long distances. "When they grieve, it's like we grieve," Qaamina said. "So when the whale was killed it was probably giving out a message— danger now." He paused, his face sad. "And these waters are supposed to be their home."

Like Alberta Thompson, the more traditional Nuu-chah-nulth now face a Tribal Council angered by their dissent. But there is a big difference. The Nuu-chah-nulth Tribe is located in Canada and the Canadian government is still opposed to hunting whales. So far, Canada lends little support to the boasts of some tribes that they, too, will return to whaling. Ironically, Canada, which is still protecting gray whales off their coasts, is not an official member of the IWC. While the United States, which has supported and sanctioned the Makah whale hunt, is a member of the IWC, which is officially committed to an international ban on whaling.

In the fall of 1999, Dotti Chamblin's brother, Makah elder Clifford (Bill) Johnson, Jr. who is known as Da-Dow-ith-Bic (Speaker of the People) granted an interview to the Mohegan Tribe based in Connecticut for their official newspaper, *Ni Ya Yo*. Initially in favor of the whale hunt, Da-Dow-ith-Bic is now highly critical of the way tribe members conducted themselves during the hunt.

As a young man he was trained in the sacred ways of the whale hunt. When he witnessed the Makah whale hunt and how the hunters killed the whale, he was disappointed. "Culturally speaking, we've opened a can of worms," admitted Da-Dow-ith-Bic.

Unlike their ancestors, the modern-day Makah whalers did not paddle out to meet the whale, but instead were towed by their support motorboat. In their pursuit and search for a whale, they used cell phones and spotters from helicopters. Lest they be towed out to a dangerous sea by a mortally wounded, harpooned whale, the crew used antitank guns. And when the whale sank to the bottom from taking water through her mouth, the U.S. Coast Guard retrieved the whale with the use of heavy wenching equipment. Where was the tradition in this whale hunt? Where was the cultural subsistence?

"Let's do it the cultural way in the old and ancient ways of our people," Da-Dow-ith-Bic asked of his own people. "Let's do that, but they're not doing it."

In October 1999, the Parker family of the Makah Tribal Council officially laid a harpoon in their canoe to signal their intent to hunt another whale during the fall migration. The Tribal Council spoke of several different families conducting separate whale hunts. There is still much inner turmoil among the Makah. Throughout the winter migration of 1999 while the whaling crews practiced in their canoe, no whale was harpooned. Perhaps it was because of rough weather and waters; or perhaps it was because the Makah were reflecting upon their next course of action in their complicated future with the gray whale.

After meeting in November with Alberta Thompson and other conservationists, Washington State Governor Gary Locke announced his opposition to the Makah hunt. He will explore whether or not the state can stop the hunting of resident whales since these mammals are officially protected under state laws. There is much dispute about whether the whale taken in the spring of 1999 was a Friendly or a resident whale— one who lives in Neah Bay part of the year.

According to Jim Darling of West Coast Whale Research Foundation who has studied resident gray whales off nearby Vancouver Island since the 1970s, any whale taken before December 1 for the fall migration and before April 1 for the spring migration will be a resident, not a migrating whale. Perhaps the whale will also be a Friendly. "Hunting the resident whales will not threaten the entire gray whale herd," Darling warned. "But it may well threaten the resident population."

If Governor Locke does declare that these whales are residents, it will be the first time the state has claimed the grays as its own, thereby taking a stand against the federal government's sponsoring the Makah's return to whaling. This could become a states' rights versus federal rights battle. Whatever the next step may be, the precedent has been set: fourteen other tribes along the West Coast have signaled their intent to return to whaling. The new century begins as the old century did—the world again gone whaling.

And what of Alberta and her family? If she had known what would befall them all, would she still have committed herself to carrying so many other Makah with her and speaking out for the whale? If she had known that her little dog Mia who never strayed far from her trailer would be found far from home, run over, and killed on a reservation road; if she had known that the Tribal Council would evict her daughter Tracy from her home on tribal land and force her family to relocate as retaliation against her mother's public anti-whaling stance; if Alberta had known she would be fired from her job at the Makah Senior Center for supposedly "proselytizing" against the hunt; if she had known her grandsons would be beaten up in school; if she had known her grandson's wife Amelia would see her newborn child denied any tribal rights and privileges; if Alberta had known that she would receive death threats and the imminent prospect of being stripped of her tribal membership and benefits—would this elder also fall silent, too fragile for dissent?

"I know who I am," Alberta told me. "And I know the whale."

Two conflicting images have imprinted in my mind like a split screen. In one picture, there are young men in a canoe leaning very near a gray whale whose eye turns trustingly toward theirs just as the harpoon strikes her head. In the other picture are three young boys and their grandmother leaning, arms outstretched, eager to touch a gray whale with their hopeful hands. Sometimes the tension of holding these two images is unbearable. I am tempted to only look at one image. But I know that both pictures are true.

In a far-off and no longer isolated coastal village, there is a new chapter being written about the history between the gray whale and Makah. It is written in water and blood, in words and stories, in the hearts of elders and the hands of hunters. Who knows what three young boys on a boat reaching out to touch a gray whale will do one day in this new century—when what we now say and do becomes their history?

Hunters of the Whale

This is the story of a trust forged, betrayed, and bewildered—yet not quite broken. In the summer of 1998, the tribe's whaling crew practiced daily in a thirty-two-foot cedar canoe for their highly controversial and federally sponsored whale hunt off the far tip of the Northwest Coast. Anti-whaling protesters streamed into Neah Bay and the Makah tribe itself was divided about the whale hunt.

On such a small reservation with only six hundred full-time residents and two thousand years of a shared, complex history, rumors abounded. Some feared that the whaling crew—who had much difficulty paddling the turbulent waters—would scrap their traditional craft and instead hunt the whale with motorboats. Others worried that the crew was not spiritually or technically prepared for such a strenuous, soul-stirring hunt because of alleged drug and alcohol abuse by some of the crew members. In addition, there was much complicated infighting among long-feuding Makah families who clashed over which songs and ceremonies were proper for the whale hunt. Traditionally, the preparations and rituals surrounding the whale hunt were passed down secretly through the generations, which has resulted in present day confusion as well as lost rituals.

Standing in the center of the canoe and the eye of this storm, was Micah McCarty, 27, the young man many believed would be chosen to throw the first harpoon. Micah is the great grandson of the last Makah whaler, Hishka, who passed on to Micah's father, John McCarty, the stories of the whale hunt. If there were any spiritual spokesmen for a volatile and often angry whaling crew, it was Micah and John. John had been the executive director of the tribe's whaling commission. However, he resigned after being forced out by those on the Tribal Council who were more interested in modern technology than traditional whaling practices.

While some whaling crew members were belligerent and seemed to enjoy posing with the bazooka-sized, .50-caliber antitank gun to the eager press and an outside world appalled by their unpopular hunt, Micah and his father spoke with a reverence about the spiritual aspects of the ancient bond between the Makah and gray whale.

"To me, I'm like the last will and testament of my ancestors," Micah told a *New York Times Magazine* reporter in August 1998. Reiterating his concern that the hunt be respectful and not sacrilegious, Micah was in strict spiritual and physical training to prove he was worthy of this first hunt. His training included rigorous jogging, paddling, and cleansing. "There's an old saying that the whale chooses the whaler," Micah told *The Times*, "and I want to be honorable enough to be chosen by the whale."

As already polarized lines were drawn so taut that even reporters feared violence from covering the imminent fall hunt, Micah and John McCarty emerged as moderates. Cautiously and calmly, the father and son balanced many of the more militant whaling crew members. The Makah Tribal Council was flush with its expected "win" of a whaling quota at the fall International Whaling Committee (IWC). Hundreds of media people camped out at the reservation awaiting the photo op of the new century's Indian Wars.

Most of the media, especially from outside Washington State, indulged in the usual polarities of Indian versus environmentalists. There were a few exceptions, such as Lynda Mapes of *The Seattle Times* and Paul Shukovsky of *The Seattle Post-Intelligencer* who spent months carefully interviewing and reporting on the acrimonious and complicated factions, both within and without the tribe.

What nobody was reporting, because it was behind-the-scenes, was the five years of quiet negotiations between moderate Makah and moderate environmentalists. Their hope was to form a bond based on trust, not positions. Together, they tried to see past the present disarray and dark forces gathering on both sides, to a time when mutual trust, not treaties, might be made.

In early August 1998, an anti-whaling activist meeting in the fishing town of Port Angeles, Washington was the scene of a near riot when pro-whaling Makah tribal members showed up uninvited. Will Anderson of Progressive Animal Welfare

Society (PAWS) moderated the panel, joined by panel participants Makah elder Alberta Thompson, Toni Frohoff, Ph.D., a consultant for The Humane Society of the United States (HSUS), and Ben White of the Animal Defense League (ADL).

Honored in the United States and internationally, Makah anti-whaler, Alberta Thompson, often returned to a grim, but familiar scene at home—threats from pro-whaling tribal members and censorship from the Makah Tribal Council. She was about to lose her job at the Makah Senior Center for initiating discussions between tribal elders and members of anti-whaling groups. Alberta was growing weary of the prejudice directed against her by the Makah Tribal Council and others pushing for the fall hunt.

As Alberta sat on that Port Angeles anti-whaling panel, she seemed beyond exhaustion. Stoically, she gazed up past a mostly anti-whaling audience to eye familiar Makah who lined the back of the room, their faces hard and accusing. Yet for all their outrage, the pro-whaling Makah seemed anxious. They were at the meeting uninvited and no one knew what to expect. This was the first time Native and non-Native groups on opposing sides had met face-to-face in one room.

"This is about me!" one of the Makah women in the back of the room shouted out. "This is about the whale!"

In the small auditorium of several hundred people, the most palpable emotion running through the crowd was fear; fear of the unknown, of what was to come, of each other. Distrust and despair ran deeper than the historic bitterness between Native and non-Native. This bleakness told me that any day now, maybe even that night at the meeting, there would be someone who crossed the tense boundaries and instigated violence.

It was so familiar. This anger from hardliners on both sides of the issue, fanned by the media, anticipated by even peaceful protesters, and in an eerie way egged on by the federal government's continual exploitation of a small tribe's fractured culture. Nothing unites like a common enemy, and that night in Port Angeles, everything had conspired to make enemies easy to identify.

Angry Makah shouted and disrupted Will Anderson's patient explanations of why many people opposed a return to whaling. "I've tried to be respectful to the Makah tribe," Will began, "but these whales are not the same whales the Makah's ancestors hunted. Whale watching has given millions of people a new appreciation for this intelligent and unique species who already face so much jeopardy. We need to make decisions based on who the whales are now to us. What responsibility do we have to protect and preserve them for the future?"

Heckled and shouted down during his speech, Will was clearly frustrated and reminded the pro-whaling Makah that they had not been invited to this meeting. He warned that he might have to call security, at which point the Makah at the back of the room shouted even louder.

"But we're hungry!" a Makah woman screamed.

In this middle-aged woman's fierceness, I felt a hunger far beyond physical subsistence. There is poverty, high unemployment, and poor health on the Makah reservation, including rampant diabetes, a travail for many tribal peoples. Perhaps this Makah woman was talking about a hunger that may never be truly sated—the hunger for what had been stolen from them. Was she talking about a hunger for pride, for tribal identity, and respect from within the tribe as well as from the outside world? Maybe this woman was remembering that once long ago, the gray whales had put an end to all hunger. Might the whales once again save her people?

"But is it the whale meat you really need now?" someone in the audience engaged the Makah woman. "Or is it the whale?"

The Makah woman turned on him and cried out, "We're just hungry, that's all! And we don't make friends with our food!"

The entire auditorium erupted in a shouting match as pro-whaling Makah streamed into the audience and engaged in heated arguments with attendees. All semblance of a forum disappeared as everyone yelled and talked at once.

As a pro-whaler and an environmentalist screamed at each other, their faces close, their bodies tense, I hunkered down in my seat. All I wanted to do was escape this angry scene, but then I saw two images at the front of the room that held my attention: One was Alberta Thompson being harangued by a Makah man yelling, "You're liars. You're all liars!" The other was the forlorn sight of Micah McCarty standing in the front row near where he and his father had sat quietly listening to all sides before the melee erupted.

Bewildered, Micah tentatively held his Makah drum in front of him like a shield. He had carved his own drum after a long apprenticeship to a master carver, his cousin, Spencer McCarty, who was now a pro-whaler. Micah had painted his traditional Makah drum with his own dream images, and a black-and-red whale who had a large eye that seemed to gaze at the chaos with sorrow and dismay. I, too, had a Makah drum similar to Micah's that had been made by Spencer McCarty. It had hung on my wall at home for nearly a decade prior to this meeting—a prophetic connection of my involvement with the Makah.

Unlike the pro-whalers holding forth at the back of the room, clearly intent on disrupting the meeting, the McCartys had come to talk, to explain, to seek some understanding outside the tribe. "I believe that man," Micah nodded to Ben White on the panel. "He invited us to talk… " Micah's voice was drowned out by the shouting match around him.

Courtesy and compassion departed as the auditorium rang with shouts and curses. Many moderate Makah and conservationists had hoped to talk with each other, but this seemed unlikely. From my long interviews with Makah elders such as Alberta Thompson, I had learned that there was a "silent majority" on the reservation who were afraid to speak out in the presence of the more adamant pro-whalers.

Tentatively I approached Micah McCarty. "I'd like to hear what you have to say," I told him. "Please talk, if you can."

Around us, the room seemed to roil and swirl, but Micah and John McCarty, environmentalist Ben White, and I talked with our heads close together.

"This is going on today," Micah began in a soft voice, "because at the time of the treaties [in 1855] it was only three years after a major smallpox epidemic obliterated a village of our people."

After this great epidemic, two thirds of the Makah tribe were dead. Before contact, the Makah's population was estimated at between two thousand and four thousand. By the late nineteenth century, the number was under one thousand, and by 1910, there were as few as 360 living Makah. For Micah and the Makah, this history continues to be a living and terrible legacy of what can result when the Makah have contact with outsiders.

Micah continued, "Stecowilth—his name means 'gray whale'—was concerned the government was taking away our way of life. They wanted to move us to the cape [Cape Flattery] and everyone was afraid that life was going to change forever. Stecowilth said, 'I want the sea. That is my country.' And so we got our fishing, seal, and whale hunting rights."

It is impossible for those of us who are non-Indian to fathom the fear that a living history of genocide has left, even in today's generation. But ironically enough fear was something all sides shared as the first whale hunt neared. There was so much at stake for both humans and whales.

In a later conversation, John McCarty would note that by the 1920s—long before the rest of the world declared a moratorium on hunting the gray whale—the Makah elders voluntarily stopped hunting the whale. They were gravely concerned about the dwindling grays along the coast. "A good hunter never hunted an animal to extinction," McCarty explained firmly. He was referring to the Yankee whaling ships led by Captain Charles Scammon who by the mid-1800s violated even the gray whale birthing lagoons, slaughtering mothers and calves. By 1874, an estimated 10,000 to 11,300 gray whales had been killed by Yankee whalers off the Pacific Coast. By that time, many believed gray whales were all but extinct.

Since then, thanks to the voluntary hunting moratorium by the Makah, and later, the federal Endangered Species Act, the gray whale rebounded. But there were still many threats, including pollution and a proposed salt works to be built by Mitsubishi in San Ignacio Lagoon, Mexico, which scientists worldwide believe would destroy this fragile habitat.

"We Makah are very concerned about the survival for the next generations of the gray whale," John McCarty said, expressing a fear that many felt. "We want to do this hunt right with dignity and tradition—not to just kill a whale and have it float up spoiled on the beach. We have to do this hunt like the ancestors and bring that whale back up onto the beach for all the people."

Listening to Micah and John McCarty tell their stories at that Port Angeles meeting, and during many future conversations, I learned that they, too, loved the whale. And this mutual bond was a beginning between us.

That bond was called upon when Ben White, a long-time activist for Native American as well as animal rights, leaned toward Micah at the Port Angeles meeting and said, "Listen, what I learned about nature I learned from your people. You taught me a way to look in the animal's eye—that there's a person in there. After I saw that, I couldn't kill animals, I had to protect them."

"Haven't you heard about the food chain?" interrupted the Makah woman who had earlier shouted out her hunger.

"And haven't you heard us ask your Tribal Council again

and again just to sit down and talk with us?" another conservationist pleaded with her. "They've refused our every request."

Micah was about to begin again when he was interrupted by a lawyer the Makah Tribal Council had hired to represent them in their quest to return to whale hunting. "Who are you?" the attorney demanded, frowning at my tape recorder.

When I told him my name, his frown deepened. "Don't talk to her!" he angrily advised the McCartys. "She's a nature writer who does essays for *The Seattle Times*."

We were all stunned into silence by the lawyer's demands. And in that moment it was as if we all looked at each other for the first time. I saw before me in Micah a young man with his long black hair pulled back in a ponytail, his dark eyes as serious and eloquent as his words. Now, he held his hand-carved drum solidly in front of him as if protecting his heart from the onslaught. Yet, even amid the loud shouting, he remained soft-spoken and thoughtful, like a statesman. Next to him, John McCarty's weathered face was somber, showing the same bone-deep weariness I'd seen growing over the last two years in another Makah elder, Alberta Thompson.

In that instant, I wondered, *What did the McCartys see when they studied me*? Was their lawyer right to warn them away from talking to this fair-skinned, silver-haired woman with her tape recorder held tentatively toward them? Could they have recognized in me the daughter of generations of hunters, a girl who had grown up on a national forest eating nothing but wild game? Could they see my own mixed blood heritage from Cherokee, Seminole, and French Canadian?

Whatever we saw in each other was enough to override the lawyer's command that they silence themselves. Micah calmly took up again, "We just want to be clearly understood," he said.

Again the Caucasian lawyer, hired by the Makah, interrupted our fragile dialogue to talk right over the top of John McCarty's head to Ben White. "Listen," he said, as if the McCartys were not there at all, "these are simple people...."

"How dare you patronize them?" Ben demanded incredulously. "These are not simple people. How can you say that when they're standing right here? I don't want to talk to you. I want to talk to the Makah."

This seemed to break the stranglehold the lawyer had tried to impose, but we knew that we could not have any real conversation amidst such turmoil. So I asked the McCartys, "Would you meet again with a few of us to try and seek some common ground?"

"Yes," they said firmly.

At the end of the meeting, I stayed a little longer to talk with the McCartys. By the time I was ready to leave, I had lost track of my companions. Micah and I walked to the parking lot together and unknowingly I ended up in the midst of the Makah whaling crew as they encircled Micah. The crew held Micah in high esteem and they considered him the spiritual spokesman for them. Soon we were all laughing and joking together as the whaling crew teased one another. Suddenly I became aware that I was not only an outsider, but also the only woman. Traditionally, whaling is the strict province of Makah men. Yet, despite these differences, in that brief interaction I felt strangely at ease with these men who would be the hunters of the whale.

For a moment, I was confused with how comfortable I felt. It was as if I'd found myself dropped down someplace I didn't belong. But as I heard their gruff, masculine taunts to each other, their playful struts and claims to victory, their boasts about their imminent hunt, I felt myself suddenly returned to my own childhood. All my life I have been surrounded by my father, himself mixed-blood, and his talk of hunting. Sometimes I accompanied my father and his hunting buddies as they set up camp for their deer or elk hunts. They were always successful, and I had spent my childhood eating the wild, sweet game of these hunts, torn between my love for the animal and my love for my father—who had confused me. He was the one who had taught me to love and study animals.

Nothing was simple anymore. Nothing was easy now. To make this conflict an either/or situation, the "Indian versus the environmentalist," was simplistic, and not true. All I knew was that we were building a bridge between seeming opposites who still had much to say to each other.

The following week on August 21, 1998, four of us continued our dialogue on the Makah reservation. "We are among the more moderates of the tribe," Micah had confided when we first agreed to this meeting. This marked the first time a whaling crew member, Micah McCarty, had agreed to sit down and talk with representatives of whale conservation groups. Marine biologist Toni Frohoff, and Ben White of the ADL, joined Micah and myself.

Micah met us at the door and invited us into his father's home, although John McCarty did not join us that day. We all recognized that this was an historic meeting and the openness and courtesy on all sides contained us. Just as we walked into the living room, a nightly news clip showed Micah and his fellow whaling crew members vigorously paddling their canoe in training for their imminent fall hunt. We all sat down with Micah's sister Maggie to watch the news. Despite the import of the meeting, in that moment there was a familiar sense that we had simply "come calling" like far-flung neighbors.

Micah pointed out the sleek contours of the ancestral canoe, "The Hummingbird," carved by a Makah under guidance from the Nuu-chah-nulth tribe, long known for their paddling prowess. Later Micah would tell us that many traditional canoes such as "Trying to Get There" were named for the whale hunt. In the past, Makah whaling chiefs had polished their names, increasing their reputation for humility and generosity with names such as "The One Who Makes the Whale Blow on the Beach" and "Always Comes Back with the Whale."

When the newscaster reported on expected protests and violence in the upcoming annual summer event, Makah Days, the mood darkened in that living room still bright with the Northwest's evening summer light.

"Look," Micah said, noting that a whaling crewman's face was blurred on the screen. "He asked them to not show his face." The Makah crew had gotten anonymous death threats.

And the Makah well remember a history of threats that have plagued this country's Native peoples—from government sanctioned massacres to stolen homelands and attempts to annihilate Native languages, traditions, and cultures.

After the newscast, we settled in to listen to Micah. Maggie sliced and passed around warm bread, creating an air of openness. "It goes back to the great famine," Micah began. "We were here before the last Ice Age. A man went to a mountain to pray for starvation to come to an end. That's when Thunderbird brought the whales to all the beaches. This changed the Ice Age, brought warmth back to the land. The whales beached themselves for us. They saved the people from death by hunger."

For more than an hour Micah explained the history of whaling while we listened. After a long pause, Ben said, "This is a tragedy that we're at odds with the Makah when we share so much. Don't you think we're all being used here, suckered? While big business and big governments make deals that have more to do with U.S. free-trade policies with Japan and Norway than with caring about either the Makah or the whales?"

Ben has risked much of his life in defense of other species. Where Ben has the passionate and philosophic stance of a spiritual warrior, Micah is a young statesman of his tribe and an ambassador for the Makah. He has a dignity and authority that belie his 27 years. And an ability to listen graciously while others speak.

Ben told a story of living for three days and nights up in an ancient cedar in the Dosewallips rainforest in Washington State to protest the cutting of old-growth trees. "After you're up there in the treetops for days, you notice things," Ben said thoughtfully. "Every evening at dusk there is this surprising shiver that runs through all the trees. You don't just sense it, you can see the trees tremble like with wind. Then someone told me it is the trees themselves going through their daily change—from breathing out to breathing in. And this kind of consciousness, aliveness, we all share with each other and the animals as well."

Micah nodded knowingly: "We see the whales as beings. We even have ways of addressing the whales, and their ancestors, too." Then he lamented, "But so many of the Makah's old whaling songs and dances have been lost. We have tried to remember them. I want us to be one with the whale in spirit." Micah paused, then gravely added, "I will tell you that I don't know what I will do if, when we get out there and I look into the eye of the whale, I see that our crew is not in the spirit—not cleansed and ready in the old ways to take the whale. I don't know what I will do."

For a long while we all sat in silence. Studying Micah's almost bowed head, I had a sharp pang of fear for him. What would be more dangerous for him in this modern whale hunt—going against his own whaling crew or censoring his own doubts about their spiritual readiness to meet the whale as had their ancestors?

"I have seen things within my own tribe that make me sad," Micah continued, referring to past Tribal Council corruption and politics. Then, as to forgive such failings, he added, "We have suffered so much. And we still are oppressed. Many people cannot forget or see past this. Some Makah only see an ongoing retaliation, a brutal drive by outsiders to assimilate us and tell us what to do."

As he spoke, I thought about what a Native Hawaiian woman once told me: "When you study the history of indigenous peoples, you also have to reckon with neo-colonialism. This is the third or fourth generation of Native people, some of whom have taken on the rapacious ways of the first colonizers. These neo-colonials—even though they are Native—turn upon their own more traditional people. And this begins yet another cycle of persecution, but from within."

Her explanation made perfect sense in relationship to the Makah. The very U.S. government that once persecuted Native peoples, now supports certain corrupt tribal councils on the mainland. "It's happening everywhere," the Hawaiian woman observed. "The split is between tribal traditionalists devoted to the old ways of knowing and the natural world; and contemporary, economically driven tribal councils."

I thought about elder Alberta Thompson who was still bravely speaking against the whale hunt on behalf of many frightened elders. She had just been fired from her job of fifteen years at the Makah Senior Center by the Tribal Council. The council sent a memo citing her helping another elder make telephone contact with a representative from the environmental group, Sea Shepherd, as grounds for her dismissal. What would she do now to make a living? And if the council made good their threat to drop her from the tribal rolls, who would pay for her food and health care?

As Micah spoke I wondered if one day after he'd completed his environmental law studies at the Northwest Indian College in Bellingham, he might be welcomed back to his own tribe as a future leader like his father. He certainly had the vision and intelligence to grasp the complexities of government. He also had the compassion. Then Micah offered, "I've really been thinking about the common ground between us. We're losing so much," he continued, referring to all of us who care about the environment. "Our fisheries are in bad shape so that many fishermen are not making ends meet. I, too, share your concern about Mitsubishi salt mines in the Baja gray whale birthing lagoons." For another hour or so we talked about the threats to timberlands, watersheds, salmon, wolves—the same problems that affect all peoples of the Northwest.

Then we returned to the subject of the imminent whale hunt. Micah concluded, "Like you, the Makah are trying to balance our spiritual lessons with our material existence. And we're trying to keep our own identity."

I thought back to the recent Port Angeles meeting and one overwhelming image that rose above the chaos. Whether they were wearing cetacean jewelry or T-shirts with gray whales emblazoned on their backs, or like Micah, carrying a drum with gray whales in a family design—all the people in that auditorium were identifying with whales, but from different perspectives.

At the kitchen table, Toni and Micah began swapping whale-sighting stories. For the first time, both sides told their stories of this shared identity with the whale. Micah spoke about journeying to Hawaii to swim with the same wild dolphins both Toni and I had studied. Toni talked about her winter Baja trip to the birthing and breeding grounds of grays.

"We want the whales to do well and stay healthy," Micah agreed. "It is in keeping with our traditions and the way of our ancestors."

Toward the end of our five hours together, most of it spent huddled around the kitchen table, we found ourselves considering an alternative—a nonlethal, ceremonial Makah whale hunt. We wondered if this imagined annual ceremonial hunt might become as successful as the Seattle salmon homecoming powwow and celebration, which attracts more than sixty thousand people every September, a majority of them tribal peoples from throughout North America.

At this ceremonial Makah whale hunt, we wondered whether the Makah might increase their proud reputation worldwide: That the Makah were not the killers, but the Keepers of the Whale. "I have had this vision," Micah said with conviction.

We took our leave of each other with the pledge to meet again. As we walked away, Toni leaned towards me and quietly admitted, "I don't know what to do now, except keep protecting the whale. But now I also hold dear one who holds the harpoon."

During the early fall of 1998, as preparations for the first whale hunt intensified and tensions escalated, the quiet and fragile coalition between the moderate Makah represented by the McCartys and the conservationists strengthened. Our dialogue and personal trust in each other had grown, even as newspaper headlines screamed of "a recipe for disaster" on the high seas when those protecting the whales and those hunting the whales clashed.

Before the hunt polarized everyone even further, now seemed the time to give voice to this fledgling dialogue seeking common ground. The McCartys agreed that an article in *The Seattle Times* on what some of us fondly referred to as "the Kitchen Roundtable" would be helpful. I admired the McCarty's courage to go public with their ideas, which were in conflict with the Makah Tribal Council. It was as if through the newspaper forum, they could make audible many of the silenced voices among their tribe. The McCartys knew that the world as well as their own tribal members would be listening. When I asked John McCarty whether printing this story might jeopardize him or his son within his own tribe, John said simply, "We are who we are."

I read the entire article over the speaker phone to the McCartys and other tribal members unknown to me who gathered to hear what I had written for *The Seattle Times.* Journalists rarely check more than their quotes with interviewees, but I felt it was more important to continue the trust we had carefully built by letting the McCartys hear all I had written. After all, it was their story. Also, I did not want to put them in any danger with their own people or others who might be more militant.

After I finished reading the entire text, there was a long silence and I imagined the other Makah gathered around the speakerphone. *Would it float?* I wondered. *Would they back out in fear of possible repercussions?* After all, they were putting out the idea of a hunt in which no whale was killed, but ancient traditions and an interspecies bond still honored. Anxiously, I awaited their comments.

At last Micah softly responded, "You have done us honor. We are not afraid."

"Thank you for your courage," I said, and let out a long withheld breath. "And for your vision."

On October 2, 1998 the article ran in *The Seattle Times* under the headline, "Makah Have Another Way to Hunt and Honor Whales." Reaction was immediate and unexpected. One Makah told me anonymously that if the ceremonial and nonlethal whale hunt idea would be voted upon in Neah Bay at that moment, "it would have unanimous support on the reservation."

Some of the Makah were unhappy with the whaling crew. One member had been seen breaking the strict purification and cleansing regimen of a Makah whaler by drinking beer in the midst of preparations for the sacred hunt. There were more rumors about drug abuse among some whaling crew members. Mixing substance abuse and antitank weaponry was a dangerous cocktail, especially when the world was watching.

The publication of the McCarty essay happened to coincide with an embarrassing and very public capsizing of the whaling canoe into cold waters during a practice run. The media also recorded the whaling canoe being towed around Neah Bay by a support motorboat. The public reacted with strong disapproval that the crew was relying upon modern, rather than traditional skills.

In those televised video clips, I was surprised not to see Micah in his usual position in the whaling canoe. Later he announced publicly that he left the whaling crew mid-hunt because he wanted to return to college in nearby Bellingham. But privately, it was a different story.

The personal reasons why Micah left the whaling crew remain within his family and are inviolate. A variety of anti-whalers claimed to have influenced Micah's decision. These claimants included Michael Kundu of Sea Shepherd, an environmental organization much reviled on the reservation for its intimidation tactics, which rivaled the Makah Tribal Council's own hard-line style. But I believe that the McCartys had come to this decision long before any dialogue with out-siders, including our Kitchen Roundtable.

Pondering Micah's choice to leave the whaling canoe, I remembered his quiet face in August when we sat at his father's kitchen table. His words haunted me. "I don't know what I will do if, when I get out there and look into the eye of the whale, I see that our crew is not in the spirit, not cleansed and ready in the old ways to take the whale—I don't know what I will do."

I do believe that at the time, if Micah had taken his place with the whaling crew and thrown the first harpoon, the act may have shattered his soul. Many whalers have reported that when a gray is struck with a harpoon, the whale lets out a banshee's wail that will haunt a man for the rest of his life. The only balance to such a cry from a wild animal would be the firm conviction of a whole tribe's spiritual subsistence.

With their spiritual center gone, the whaling crew fell into the hands of angry young men led by Wayne Johnson, the crew captain, and driven by members of the Tribal Council, such as the Parker family. Wayne was more accomplished with his antitank gun practice than with press conferences. Again and again he stumbled publicly when explaining what was the true meaning of this hunt for his people. Under the tutelage of the Tribal Council and Wayne, the Makah hunt focused more on an exercise of "in-your-face treaty rights" than the restoration of spiritual and cultural whaling traditions.

Wayne enjoyed posing with the .50-caliber, armor-piercing antitank gun—twice as powerful as an elephant gun—for media photos. He summarized the spectacle surrounding the whale hunt for *The Seattle Times* as, "Big whales, big waves, big guns, and a lot of crazy people." If his crew were threatened by protesters, such as the Sea Shepherd, who were known for ramming illegal whaling vessels, Wayne promised, "If they ram us, we'll ram them."

In the fall of 1998 the whaling crew did not succeed in taking a whale. In the background, there was a frenzy of confidential negotiations and private presentations by environmentalists to the Tribal Council. Ben White led a coalition of concerned environmental organizations looking for long-term economic alternatives to whale hunting for the Makah. He stressed that all plans must be both pro-Makah and pro-whale. Among the offers by moderate, grassroots environmental groups was buying back land for the Makah that the federal government had once taken from the tribe. There were also offers to create programs that increased economic health for the Makah, including whale watching, reforestation, wind generation, and educational opportunities.

Ben White was highly suspicious of the U.S. federal government's involvement. "We have to ask this," Ben declared. "Why is the U.S. government behind this hunt? Why did the Commerce Department give $310,000 to the Makah to sell this idea? Could it be that open war on wildlife is being thrown to the Native people as an affirmative action plum instead of serious redress for land issues and genocide?"

The Tribal Council rejected any proposals for alternative economic development other than whale hunting. This included a $3 million offer from communications mogul Craig McCaw who had financed other whale conservation projects. In the face of these offers, the Makah Tribal Council strictly limited the issue to an exercise of treaty rights, repeatedly stating the Makah whaling rights were not for sale. The Tribal Council continually narrowed the dialogue others were trying to open.

Amid all of the tension, Toni Frohoff and I journeyed several times more to the reservation to meet with Micah and John McCarty. We were also invited to meet Micah's mother, Anne Lunt. John and Anne had divorced, but they keep a close, cordial relationship with each other and their shared children. Anne, a Caucasian woman from Boston, is both a long-time Indian rights activist and a follower of the Ba'hai spiritual tradition. Her life emphasis is on finding inner and global peace. She had feared for her son's safety on the Makah whaling canoe; she had also seen much on the Makah reservation to give her concern for her ex-husband, her daughter, and her son's welfare.

Reflecting both his mother's spiritual expansiveness and his father's Native traditions, Micah searched for his own answers in the divisive issue of Makah whaling. He and his father were not helped in this complicated path by a betrayal that came from outside the tribe.

Throughout the autumn of 1998, we quietly arranged for another whale watch with Makah and conservationists. The McCartys had agreed to come together in trust again, this time on the water. More than thirty Makah tribal members excitedly signed up for this whale watch, right in the midst of the whaling crew's final preparations for a whale hunt. The whale watch was intended to be another gesture for creating more understanding between Makah and environmentalists. Only a handful of people, aside from the Makah, knew of this event planned for late October 1998. We kept the whale watch plans quiet in order to avoid a media circus and the potential for violence.

Happily, we were preparing to meet again and enjoy the autumn whale watch on Neah Bay. But in the final weeks all our efforts fell apart. On October 16, John McCarty called me in a fury. Someone in a non-profit environmental organization had leaked our whale watch plans, not to the press, but to a Hollywood philanthropist who is involved with environmental issues. In a flagrant disregard for the McCartys or any grassroots conservationists who had labored for almost four years to build this fragile trust, this philanthropist had unilaterally decided to dispatch a letter by fax to all 150 tribes on the West Coast. In the fax he hailed the McCartys as heroes for opposing their tribe's hunt and advised all tribes to follow their example. It was a classic example of a white man dictating "The Way" to Native peoples without any respect or knowledge of the Makah's complex history or culture, or that such an action might be damaging to the McCartys.

After the betrayal of our shared whale watch by the environmental organization, the trust between the McCartys and those engaged in common ground dialogues was only partly restored. The McCartys were gracious enough to keep inviting me to their home. But they firmly closed the doors to others. The trust first forged between these Makah moderates and representatives of environmental organizations may never again be as it once was. Yet for six months after our thwarted whale watch, those seeking a pro-Makah and pro-whale solution still continued to share ideas.

In January 1999, Micah McCarty took his place on an international panel on Makah whaling at Whales Alive on Maui. Though Micah was challenged by some marine mammal scientists and whale activists questioning the Makah decision to resume the whale hunt, he maintained his calm and contemplative presence. Over the days, our kitchen table dialogue was extended to the global stage as all sides listened to one another. Without the glare of the media awaiting violent photo ops of militant clashes or blood in the water, diplomacy and the attentiveness of mutual respect held sway.

Negotiations and offers to the Tribal Council for an alternative to the whale hunt continued up until the day before the Makah whaling crew harpooned and killed the first gray whale hunted off the North American mainland in almost a century.

On May 17, 1999, when Makah whaling crew killed a juvenile gray whale, I tried to go about my day. But I could not get out of my mind the image of that young juvenile gray looking up at the canoe so trustingly. She was only two years old. Two years before that, I had reached far out of a boat on a

Baja lagoon and touched my first gray whale calf.

Looking back on that turning point when peaceful negotiations between moderate Makah and moderate environmentalists faltered, I wonder about the other trusts that have been betrayed in two centuries of our country's struggles between indigenous people and settlers. A broken promise, an indiscretion, an honest mistake—there are so many stories that never made the history books. We hear only of the wars—the winners and losers. But what of those who battled most to understand themselves and to reconcile seeming opposites? What about those who allowed themselves troubling ambivalence and soul searching, without an easy answer? These mediators and moderates may in the end change history; but rarely are their stories heard beneath the clash and drama of violent foes.

Perhaps there will come a time when historians record and praise the stories of dialogue and negotiation, instead of simplistic pro-and-con and the either/or split that have driven historical accounts. Will we also write stories about those who ventured far away from their own comfortable positions, to imagine and understand the points of view of the Other? The peacemakers—as Chief Sealth was in the early days of the city that still bears his name—must also have their day.

In setting down this story, I wanted to conserve what I believe is best about the human spirit. That is our openness and ability to change, to learn flexibility, and to understand even contradictory or paradoxical opinions. My favorite aphorism of intelligence is "the ability to tolerate a high degree of ambiguity."

Micah McCarty now lives on the Makah reservation with his wife and their firstborn, a daughter whom they named Ianna, after the ancient Sumerian goddess who visits the underworld and returns with her soul completed by the descent.

What worlds will Micah's daughter or other Makah children find when they return from the descent into which this whale hunt has cast their tribe? On their windswept tribal lands by the sea, ancient history, and a new century must meet—as sure as the tide, but never as expected.

Trusting, Taken

Gray whale
Now that we are sending you to The End
That great god
Tell him
That we who follow you invented forgiveness
And forgive nothing

    —W.S. Merwin, "For a Coming Extinction"

A treaty has been kept and a treaty broken. The treaty that is honored is the one given the Makah tribe in 1855 to keep their whaling rights. The treaty that is broken is one of trust made between other peoples of the coast and the gray whale.

    Over the past seventy years whales have learned to trust our boats, our cries of welcome, and even our outstretched hands. In Baja, Friendly whales have allowed their newborn calves to make contact with humans. Eventually these calves migrate north, and continue to trust the treaty between humans and whales.

In Baja birthing grounds I made a promise to the gray whales to work for their protection. I stroked a mother and calf's barnacled sides and looked long into the engaging, calm eye of the mother gray whale.

The whale who approached the Makah tribal canoe in May 1999 had no history of human harm and no instinct to fear the hunters. That whale came close to a canoe because she had been taught by humans to receive kindness. Not wary, the whale expected to be made welcome. Some who had been on the scene say the whale rolled to her side to better see the people, to make the curious eye contact that many humans have witnessed with the Friendly whales.

After I witnessed the televised live kill of the juvenile gray, I went down to the shores of Puget Sound to make apology and say prayers for the passing of this young whale in our home waters. From the waves, sea lions barked like a chorus of mourners and gulls circled above calling their high wail. Within a tide pool lay black sand dollars adorned with seaweed. In memory of this first whale sacrificed, I placed a pale gardenia in the tide pool and its ripples circled outward like the mysterious circles this death will make. But I could not yet weep.

Suddenly I noticed three men walk towards me on the beach. "*Como estas?*" one asked.

"*Muy triste,*" I said. "I am very sad." Then we continued in Spanish and I told him about the death of the gray whale. He told me he was from Guadalajara and loved the sea.

"*Los ballenas Amistos?*" he said. He, too, knows of the Friendly whales in his country's birthing grounds.

"Yes," I whispered. "They think it was a Friendly who was killed by the trusting way she approached the Makah canoe."

"*Si, es muy triste,*" he lamented. Then he took something from his pocket and reached out to me.

It was an ornate carved, pine wood whale with a black eye and smiling mouth. "*Para ti,*" he said softly. "For you. And for the whale."

The synchronicity of that exchange is a mystery: That while I was on the beach to mourn the death of the gray whale, a passerby gave me a carving he had just found in a beach house he and his fellow workers were tearing down. After they left, I held the small whale in my hand and wept.

Is there any song the Makah can now sing for the whale that is greater than themselves and their own rights? It is my prayer that we will all, tribal and non-Native peoples, sit in stillness and memory of a great spirit given in trust.

Between Species

Apprenticeship
to Animal Play

In my own life I have always placed a high value on play. Once at my birthday party, a friend decorated my cake with the inscription: "I play, therefore I am." I've always considered my decade of studying and encountering dolphins, mostly in the wild, as an apprenticeship to play; to learn the lessons of another intelligent species that spends three-quarters of their lives at play. What is it about play that is so important that it has evolved into a central preoccupation for large-brained mammals, as well as other species?

In a *National Geographic* companion video to its cover story on "Animals at Play," there is an interview with Mark and Helen Atwater who run a baby gorilla orphanage in Brazzillaville on the Congo River. The couple spends much of their day—in fact, up to seven hours a day—at play to rehabilitate these orphaned gorillas before they can return them to the wild.

"Play is a real milestone," remarks Helen Atwater as she cradles a tiny gorilla named Goko. Suddenly the little orphan grins and lets out a high-pitched huffing sound.

"Is that a giggle?" asks the researcher as Goko wraps his long arms around Helen Atwater's neck and swings from her body.

"Yes," Atwater smiles. "We call it a 'gorilla giggle.' They love to be tickled."

These baby gorillas also love to be cuddled, preened, nuzzled, swung upside down, and physically adored like any human infant.

Sometimes it takes as long as a year for these orphaned gorillas to play again. "Like Goko here," says Atwater, "many of these baby gorillas have seen their mothers or their entire families murdered. They are too traumatized to play."

Teaching these baby gorillas to play again is restoring a survival skill to an endangered species. It is also a lesson our species can take to heart in a world where so many children have been traumatized by abuse, poverty, and war. The Atwaters and many other animal researchers are trying to preserve not only primates and habitat but also to remind us of what most parents know about their offspring: to play is to survive.

Whenever I want to study and expand my capacity for play I journey into the wild to encounter dolphins or whales. On a recent visit to Key West, Florida to be with a pod of wild dolphins, I also met an unusual and delightful woman, Captain Rosie. One of the few female skippers in the Keys and a marine naturalist, Captain Rose took our group of women nature writers out into the open ocean. We hoped to meet bottlenose dolphins in a nursery pod, who have played with Captain Rosie over the past two decades.

"When I first encountered this nursery pod, I didn't realize they were all female," Captain Rosie told us as she revved up her motorboat on a cold Florida winter day. We zoomed across a turquoise sea, and though it was sunny, we were bundled under patchwork quilt comforters in what Rosie called a "Florida Keys Sleigh Ride." Shouting above the wind gusts, Captain Rosie explained, "Over on the south side, you have the Swinging Singles—the bachelor pod of male bottlenose having themselves a mighty good time. But I like to spend my time with 'the girls,' even though some of these females are grandmothers now and I'm playing with their grandchildren—or grandcalves."

Captain Rosie laughed, her head thrown back, her short, dark hair styled by strong winds. Here was the wide-open, sun-wrinkled face of a grandmother herself abandoned to the call of the sea and these sister creatures she believed were her own extended family. A mother of a grown son, Rosie divides her time between the sea where she leads nature and wildlife expeditions lending others her expertise as a marine environmental educator and onshore she goes dancing almost every night.

The motorboat roared flat out like a high-speed hydroplane. Our faces were rearranged by the wind, smiles pulled taut, sunglasses and bright bandanas plastered to our heads with the gale force of our ocean flight.

"Watch the water!" Captain Rosie called out to us as we shivered against each other . "The colors are like a topographic map to tell us depths and shallows. See that dark, emerald green path? That's the deep water and the turquoise is where we might run aground. So, hang on to your hats!"

What hats we had were already blown overboard. I was reduced to my scarf double-knotted beneath my chin. Several of the other women covered their bare heads with bright blankets. We looked like an Amish quilting bee pirated by Captain Rosie from our women's work right out onto the high seas. Only one of us was warm—an editor leaned from the prow of the boat, arms flung out like a blissful, bare-bosomed masthead. No maiden she, this was the first time she'd been cool since she began menopause.

Suddenly Captain Rosie cut the motor and we trolled quietly along a luminous aqua stream of sun slanting on open sea. It was so bright, it took several moments to focus on the distant dorsal fins arching up and down in high waves. "Listen," Captain Rosie whispered. "Dolphins love music, especially waltzes. It's the four-quarter time, like music at a skating rink, *da-dum, da-dum, da-dum, dum-dum...*" Captain Rosie sang in a resonant soprano and did a perfect pirouette at the helm. She didn't even rock the boat.

Music surrounded us. A Strauss waltz echoed under the fiberglass shell of Rosie's boat like an underwater speaker sending the graceful sound vibrations through the sea to the pod. Captain Rosie was so familiar with the pod, she could identify each dolphin by the dorsal fin. We felt the rhythmic music's romantic pulses resonating up through the boat's hull and into our feet. Knees bent, we balanced with the waves of waltz and sea, laughing and swaying in perfect time to the music and rock of the boat. We had sea legs, like some hula girls, whose undulant bodies remember ancient rhythms of moontides and understand this familiar womb of water.

Suddenly, this nursery pod arched up to leap above our bow, inches away from our outstretched hands. Benevolent, unblinking eyes sought ours at mid-flight. The dolphins studied us: Were we to be trusted? Did we mean harm? Did we have bad taste in music? Would we make even tolerable dance partners?

In perfect synch, six dolphins dived back down to disappear and we were left bobbing by ourselves like wallflowers awaiting an invitation. "*Da-dum, da-dum, da-dum, dum-dum!*" Captain Rosie sang out at the top of her lovely voice.

She had told us before we left shore that her first encounter with this wild nursery pod had left her utterly changed. "They circled me underwater," she recalled. "Careful and curious. After all, they had babies to protect and humans don't have such a great record for respecting their privacy. But I just hung out there with my scuba, trying to make quiet bubbles. One of the dolphins swam right up into my face mask and simply gazed at me for what seemed like an hour. Her sonar zinged inside my body like a tuning fork, her big eye studying me with such kindness I almost cried. Then she made her decision. I was a human she could afford to meet." Captain Rosie grinned. "And now, we've all known each other so long that sometimes I can't figure out if I'm babysitting them or they're looking out for me. All I know is that they keep inviting me to dance."

Captain Rosie changed the music to a more luxurious waltz, with violins and even a sonorous cello. This seemed to delight the dolphins who suddenly shot straight up out of the water flanking our boat on both sides, then splashing under the surface in exact rhythm to the waltz. They synchronized their breathing to time with the upbeat and then dove on the down-beat. Up—exhale; inhale—down. Their open-close blowholes were percussive instruments holding the syncopated heartbeat of the song. Wave after wave of music and dolphins rising and falling until scanning the horizon was like looking at a sheet of music, and the grace, half-, and trilling notes were sleek, leaping dolphin bodies. The dolphins punctuated the music with their signature high-frequency whistles. Did these dolphins perhaps recognize that in our own way we, too, were a female pod—sisters on the sea?

Watching water dense with diving dolphins, I remembered reading once that in Australian petroglyphs there are rock pictures drawn of humans rising out like little people-bubbles birthed from the blowholes of dolphins. Some of our country's indigenous myths also credit the animals with *playing* the whole world into creation.

As the last waltz faded, the dolphins dove and disappeared as if the dance were over. Captain Rosie leaned over the helm and declared, "I only bring humans who I think will give the dolphins hope. I'm showing you to them today so that these dolphins will go back to their Swinging Single bachelor pods and say, 'Okay, guys, it's *your* turn to play with us. Let's make more love. Let's make more of *us!*"

Just as play is preparation for the challenges of later life, it is also a behavior that calls forth from us, animals and humans alike, the highest creativity and intelligence in imagining the future. Visionaries in any species are often those who play most profoundly. They look over the next hill; they find a new way of swinging from a tree to ford a river that one day might rise to a flash flood; they mate in new ways. They do not support the status quo. This play is often risky behavior for many animals, because while a dolphin is spinning, a monkey is pirouetting, a lion somersaulting or making love on the open savanna, that individual is at risk to predator—and sometimes even at risk from his or her own species.

When we play, we give up our wariness and our walls and our old structures and give over to provocative play. Some scientists believe that those who play the most in any species are also those who most advance evolution. If play were not somehow essential to evolution, why would natural selection have permitted, even promoted, such unabashed play?

Perhaps the unexplored and often undervalued territory of human and animal play is truly the final frontier that we can explore between species and within ourselves. Play is a pristine and wild preserve that begins an inward adventure and expands out into the wider world where we include others in our imagination, our invitation to play.

These days in my waterfront studio, I look up at walls adorned with photos of whales and dolphins. And I ask myself questions that restore my sense of play as survival. What if, like dolphins, each of us spent three-quarters of every day at play? What if, like baby gorillas surviving their orphan-trauma, we spent seven hours a day grooming, tickling, preening, and wrapping our loving primate limbs around each other? What if, like lions, we lie in the sunshine, our feline tails ticking off naptimes, while our offspring, the next generation, lay curled in a dreaming litter?

And what if we played with our griefs, our losses, our imaginary enemies—until just by going through the motion of play, we remember not to take ourselves so seriously. What if we sigh and let go, like people-bubbles popping out of the blowholes of dolphins as they play at making more of us? Could we make new worlds on open seas—between species?

Animal Allies

"My imaginary friend really lived once," the teenage girl began, head bent, her fingers twisting her long red hair. She stood in the circle of other adolescents gathered in my Arts and Lectures storytelling class at the summer Seattle Academy. Here were kids from all over the city—every color and class, all strangers to one another. Over the next two weeks we would become a fierce tribe, telling our own and our tribe's story.

Our first assignment was to introduce our imaginary friends from childhood. This shy fourteen-year-old girl, Sarah, caught my attention on the first day because she always sat next to me, as if under my wing. Though her freckles and stylish clothes suggested she was a popular girl, her demeanor showed the detachment of someone much too preoccupied. She never met my eye, nor did she join in the first few days of storytelling when the ten boys and four girls regaled the group with futuristic characters called Shiva and Darshon, Masters of the Universe. So far the story lines we imagined were more Pac-Man than drama. After the first two days I counted a legion of characters killed off in intergalactic battle. The settings for all these stories portrayed the earth as an environmental wasteland, a ruined shell hardly shelter to anything animal or human. One of the girls called herself Nero the White Wolf and wandered the blackened tundra howling her powerful despair; another girl was a unicorn whose horn always told the truth. All the stories were full of plagues and nuclear wars—even though this is the generation that has witnessed the fall of the Berlin Wall, the end of the Cold War. Their imaginations have been shaped by a childhood story line that anticipates the end of this world.

After three days of stories set on an earth besieged by disease and barren of nature, I made a rule: No more characters or animals could die this first week. I asked if someone might imagine a living world, one that survives even our species.

It was on this third day of group storytelling that Sarah jumped into the circle and told her story:

"My imaginary friend is called Angel now because she's in heaven, but her real name was Katie," Sarah began. "She was my best friend from fourth to tenth grade. She had freckles like me and brown hair and more boyfriends—sometimes five at a time—because Katie said, 'I *like* to be confused!' She was a real sister, too, and we used to say we'd be friends for life...." Sarah stopped, gave me a furtive glance and then gulped in a great breath of air like someone drowning, about to go down. Her voice dropped to a monotone. "Then one day last year, Katie and

I were walking home from school and a red sports car came up behind us. Someone yelled, 'Hey, Katie!' She turned... and he blew her head off. A bullet grazed my skull, too, and I blacked out. When I woke up, Katie was gone, dead forever." Sarah stopped, stared down at her feet and murmured in that same terrible monotone, "Cops never found her murderer, case is closed."

All the kids shifted and took a deep breath, although Sarah herself was barely breathing at all. "Let's take some time to write," I told the kids and put on a cello concerto for them to listen to while they wrote. As they worked, the kids surreptitiously glanced over at Sarah, who sat staring at her hands in her lap.

I did not know what to do with her story; she had offered it to a group of kids she had known but three days. It explained her self-imposed exile during lunch hours and while waiting for the bus. All I knew was that she'd brought this most important story of her life into the circle of storytellers. The story could not be ignored or *she* would be a case closed. This story lived in her, defined, and shaped her young life. Because she had given it to us, we needed to witness and receive; and perhaps tell it back to her in the ancient tradition of tribal call and response.

"Listen," I told the group as the cello faded and they looked up from their work. "We're going to talk story the way they used to long ago when people sat around at night in circles just like this one. That was a time when we still listened to animals and trees and didn't think ourselves so alone in this world. Now we're going to carry out jungle justice and find

Katie's killer. We'll call him before our tribe. All right? Who wants to begin the story?"

All the Shivas and Darshons and Masters of the Universe volunteered to be heroes on this quest. Nero the White Wolf asked to be a scout. Unicorn, with her truth-saying horn, was declared judge. Another character joined the hunt: Fish, whose translucent belly was a shining "soul mirror" that could reveal one's true nature to anyone who looked into it.

A fierce commander of this hunt was Rat, whose army of computerized comrades could read brain waves and call down lightning lasers as weapons. Rat began the questioning and performed the early detective work. Katie, speaking from beyond the earth, as Sarah put it, gave us other facts. We learned that two weeks before Katie's murder, one of her boyfriends was shot outside a restaurant by a man in the same red car—another drive-by death. So Sarah had not only seen her best friend killed at her side, but she had also walked out into a parking lot to find Katie leaning over her boyfriend's body. For Sarah, it had been two murders by age thirteen.

With the help of our myriad computer-character legions we determined that the murderer was a man named Carlos, a drug lord who used local gangs to deal cocaine. At a party Carlos had misinterpreted Katie's videotaping her friends dancing as witnessing a big drug deal. For that, Rat said, "This dude decides Katie's got to go down. So yo, man, he offs her without a second thought."

Bad dude, indeed, this Carlos. And who was going to play Carlos now that all the tribe knew his crime? I took on the role, and as I told my story I felt my face hardening into a contempt that carried me far away from these young pursuers, deep into the Amazon jungle where Rat and his computer armies couldn't follow, where all their space-age equipment had to be shed until there was only a hand-to-hand simple fate.

In the Amazon, the kids changed without effort, an easy shape-shifting to their animal selves. Suddenly there were no more Masters of the Universe with intergalactic weapons— there was instead Jaguar and Snake, Fish and Pink Dolphin. There was powerful claw and all-knowing serpent, there was Fish who could grow big and small, and a dolphin whose sonar saw past the skin. We were now a tribe of animals, pawing, running, invisible in our jungle, eyes shining in the night, seeing Carlos as he canoed the mighty river, laughing because he did not know that animals were tracking him.

All through the story, I'd kept my eye on Sarah who played the role of her dead friend. The detachment I'd first seen in her was in fact the deadness Sarah carried, the violence that had hollowed her out inside, the friend who haunted her imagination. But now her face was alive, responding to each animal's report of tracking Carlos. She hung on the words, looking suddenly very young, like a small girl eagerly awaiting her turn to enter the circling jump rope.

"I'm getting away from you," I said, snarling as I'd imagined Carlos would. I paddled my canoe and gave a harsh laugh, "I'll escape, easy!"

"No!" Sarah shouted. "Let *me* tell it!"

"Tell it!" her tribe shouted.

"Well, Carlos only thinks he's escaping," Sarah smiled, waving her hands. "He's escaped from so many he's harmed before. But I call out 'FISH!' And Fish comes. He swims alongside the canoe and grows bigger, bigger until at last Carlos turns and sees this HUGE river monster swimming right alongside him and that man is afraid because suddenly Fish turns his belly up to Carlos's face. Fish forces him to look into that soul mirror. Carlos *sees* everyone he's ever killed and all the people who loved them and got left behind. And Carlos sees Katie and me and what he's done to us. He sees everything and he knows his soul is black. And he really doesn't want to die now because he knows that he'll stare into his soul mirror forever. But Fish makes him keep looking until Carlos starts screaming he's sorry, he's so sorry. Then... Fish *eats* him!"

The animals roared and cawed and congratulated Sarah for calling Fish to mirror a murderer's soul before taking jungle justice. Class had ended, but no one wanted to leave. We wanted to stay in our jungle, stay within our animals—and so we did. I asked them to close their eyes and call their animals to accompany them home. I told them that some South American tribes believe that when you are born, an animal is born with you. This animal protects and lives alongside you even if it's far away in an Amazon jungle. Because it came into the world the same time you did, it also dies with you to guide you back into the spirit world.

The kids decided to go home and make animal masks and to return the next day wearing the faces of their chosen animal. When they came into class the next day it was as if we never left the Amazon. Someone dimmed the lights, there were drawings everywhere of jaguars and chimps and snakes. Elaborate masks had replaced the Masters of the Universe who began this tribal journey. We sat behind our masks in a circle with the lights low and there was an acute, alert energy running among us, as eyes met behind animal faces.

I realize that I, who grew up wild in the forest, who first memorized the earth with my hands, have every reason to feel this familiar animal resonance. But many of these teenagers have barely been in the woods; in fact, many inner-city kids are *afraid* of nature. They would not willingly sign up for an Outward Bound program or a backpacking trek; they don't think about recycling in a world they believe is already ruined and in their imaginations abandoned for intergalactic nomad futures. These kids are not environmentalists who worry about saving nature. And yet, when imagining an Amazon forest too thick for weapons to penetrate, too primitive for their futuristic Pac-Man battles, they returned instinctively to their animal selves. They have only seen these are animals in zoos or on television, yet there is a profound identification, an ease of inhabiting another species that portends great hope for our own species's survival. Not because nature is "out there" to be saved or sanctioned, but because nature is *in* them. The ancient, green world has never left us though we have long ago left the forest.

What happens when we call upon our inner landscape to connect with the last remaining rainforests? I believe our imagination can be as mutually nurturing as an umbilical cord between our bodies and the planet. As we told our Amazon stories over the next week of class, gathered in a circle of animal masks, we could feel the rainforest growing in that sterile classroom. Lights low, surrounded by serpents, the jaguar clan, the elephants, I'd as often hear growls, hisses, and howls as words. Between this little classroom and the vast Amazon rain-forest stretched a fine thread of story that grew thicker each day, capable of carrying our jungle meditations.

When Elephant stood in the circle and said simply, "My kind are dying out," there was outrage from the other animals.

"We'll stop those poachers!" cried Rat and Chimp. "We'll call Jaguar clan to protect you." And they did.

This protection is of a kind that reaches the other side of the world. Children's imagination is a primal force, just as strong as lobbying efforts and boycotts and endangered species acts. When children claim another species as not only their imaginary friend, but also as the animal within them—their ally—doesn't that change the outer world?

This class believes it to be so. They may be young, but their memories and alliances with the animals are very old. By telling their own animal stories they are practicing ecology at its most profound and healing level. Story as ecology—it's so simple, something we've forgotten. In our environmental wars the emphasis has been on saving species, not *becoming* them. We've fallen into an environmental fundamentalism. We call down hellfire and brimstone on the evil polluters and self-righteously strut about protecting other species as if we are gods who can save their souls.

But the animals' souls are not in our hands. Only our own souls are within our ken. It is our own spiritual relationship to animals that must evolve. Any change begins with imagining ourselves in a new way. And who has preserved their imaginations as a natural resource acutely? Not adults, who so often have strip-mined their dreams and imagination for material dross.

Those who sit behind the wheel of a Jaguar have probably forgotten the wild, black cat who first ran with them as children. Imagination is relegated to nighttime dreams, which are then dismissed in favor of "the real world." But children, like some adults, know that the real world stretches farther than what we can see—that's why they shift easily between visions of our tribal past and our future worlds. The limits of the adult world are there for these teenagers, but they still have a foot in the vast inner magic of childhood. It is this magical connection I called upon when I asked the kids to do the Dance of the Animals.

The day of the big dance I awoke with a sharp pain at my right eye. Seems my Siamese cat Ivan, who has always slept draped around my head, had stretched and his claw caught the corner of my eye. In the mirror I saw a two-inch scratch streaking from my eye like jungle make-up or a primitive face painting. "The mark of the wildcat," the kids pronounced it when I walked into the dimly lit room to be met by a circle of familiar creatures. Never in ten years had my Siamese scratched my face. I took it as a sign that the dance began in his animal dream.

I put on my cobra mask and hissed a greeting to Chimp, Rat, Jaguar, and Unicorn. Keen eyes tracked me from behind colorful masks. I held up my rain stick that was also our talking stick and called the creatures one by one into the circle. "Sister Snake!" I called. "Begin the dance!"

Slowly, in rhythm to the deep, bell-like beat of my Northwest Native drum, each animal entered the circle and soon the dance sounded like this: Boom, step, twirl, and slither and stalk and snarl and chirp and caw, caw. Glide, glow, growl, and whistle and howl and shriek and trill and hiss, hiss. Each dance was distinct—from the undulating serpent on his belly, to the dainty high hoofing of Unicorn, from the syncopated stomps of Chimp on all-fours to Rat's covert jitterbug behind the stalking half-dark Jaguar. We danced, and the humid, lush jungle filled this room.

In that story line stretching between us and the Amazon, we connected with those animals and their spirits. And in return, we were complete—with animals as soul mirrors. We remembered who we were by allowing the animals inside us to survive.

The dance is not over as long as we have our animal partners. When the kids left our last class, they still wore their masks fiercely. I was told that even on the bus they stayed deep in their animal character. I like to imagine those strong, young animals out there now in this wider jungle. I believe that Rat will survive the inner-city gangs; that Chimp will find his characteristic comedy even as his parents deal with divorce; I hope that Unicorn will always remember her mystical truthtelling horn. And as for Sarah who joined the Jaguar clan, elected as the first girl-leader over much mutinous boy-growling—Sarah knows the darkness she stalks and the nightmares that stalk her. She has animal eyes to see, to find even a murderer. Taking her catlike, graceful leave, she handed me a poem she'd written, "Now I can see in the dark," she wrote; and she signed herself, "Jaguar—future poet."

War and Peace with Wolves

In the snow-draped land of the midnight sun, I attended the fractious 1993 Alaska Wolf Summit. Called by then-governor Wally Hickel to fend off an international tourist boycott to protest Alaska's policy of aerial shooting of wolves, this summit was more circus than conservation seminar. Speaker after speaker advocated the "lethal control" of Alaska's wolves—the only population of wolves in the United States that is not threatened or endangered.

Sitting at Wolf Summit press tables lining the ice rink in that Fairbanks stadium, I was chilled by the frontier "varmint" or "nuisance animal" depiction of this majestic fellow predator. State and some federal officials—whose programs are supported mostly by hunting licenses—repeated their single-species management mantra: Increase the game for hunters, decrease the predators. At night in Wild West bars and backrooms adorned with elk, moose, and caribou trophies, wildlife officials swapped hunting stories, talking predator and prey as if playing poker with other species—but the managers held all the cards.

During the Summit days, angry Alaskans clad in orange hunter vests sat in the spectator stands and violently booed any conservationist who spoke on behalf of the wolf. When Renee Askins of the Wolf Fund described the human-led holocaust against the wolves and pleaded passionately to return the wolf to balance, the furious thunder of a thousand boots stomping on bleachers drowned out her voice.

In the mid-1990s, those of us concerned about the fate of the wild wolf in our Last Frontier could only express dismay against such Old West hostility. We dreamed of a day when our country would actually restore the wolf to its natural habitat. Now that day is come, though it is still very much in jeopardy.

In March 1995, fourteen wild, Canadian gray wolves were reintroduced to Yellowstone National Park and another seventeen wolves introduced in April 1996. To date, the program has been a huge success, both in balancing the predator-prey populations within the park and in increasing tourism. The restoration project's goal is to establish three sets of ten wolves who reproduce successfully for three successive years. After this goal is met, the wolf will be taken off the endangered species list in Idaho, Montana, and Wyoming. As of the year 2000, more than *three hundred* wolves reside in Yellowstone, with a healthy birth rate of new pups in seven packs of wolves. Since the reintroduction in 1996, both wolves and tourism are flourishing in Yellowstone with more than $10 million in tourist revenue flowing into communities surrounding the park.

But even with the popularity of the Yellowstone wolf recovery there has been much wolf mortality there since 1995—over 47 percent and all caused by humans. Yet the Yellowstone wolves have been remarkably easy on ranchers and domestic livestock because the prey populations in the park are abundant.

Of all the fears and threats surrounding the reintroduction of wolves in Wyoming, Montana, Idaho, North Carolina, Tennessee, Arizona, and now New Mexico, the truth is that wolves are still the most threatened of all. Even though there is no record of any human death from a healthy wild wolf, the public is still ignorant about the real, as opposed to the demonized, wolf of our myths. In fact, a dog bites a human in this country every thirty seconds and domesticated dogs kill thirty-two people a year. Wolves are elusive, avoid humans, and are devoted to their family packs. Humans are not the wolf's prey. Elk, deer, caribou, and other ungulate populations are.

As for livestock mortality, the Defenders of Wildlife started a program in 1987 to compensate farmers and ranchers for livestock killed by wolves. They have only had to reimburse $58,934.00 to 56 ranchers for 76 cattle and 192 sheep killed since 1987.

As Diane Boyd-Heger, a wildlife biologist who has studied wolves for many years in Glacier National Park, Arizona, and now Yellowstone, remarks, "Wolves are often a clean-up act for human hunters. Wolves don't have to work very hard because human hunters leave so many wounded animals in the woods."

Perhaps wolf control is more about understanding and controlling ourselves, rather than wolves. We can learn a great deal about family and self-regulating societies from a wolf pack. Alpha males and females are generally the only pair in a pack to give birth and the rest of the family—from subordinate males to aunts—nurture the pups.

Wolves are so loyal and social among themselves that savagery toward their own is rare. Within the family, wolf altruism is well known. In fact, the concept of pack loyalty was used against the wolves in the government extermination policies. In 1914 and the early days of Yellowstone National Park, avid hunter Teddy Roosevelt declared wolves to be "sores of terror and destruction." The Park Service made war on wolves. Park officials would tie a wolf cub to a tree and torture the animal, in order to bring the entire pack out to defend its young. Then the Park Service simply opened fire on the family pack. This extermination policy was so lethal that by 1926, the last Yellowstone wolf was gunned down.

After the successful 1995 Yellowstone reintroduction, there was an echo of President Roosevelt's bias in the 1997 legal decision by Judge William Downes to forcibly remove all the restored Yellowstone wolves. In a lawsuit by The Farm Bureau, a wealthy, anti-environmental agribusiness lobbying group, Judge Downes ruled that the reintroduction was illegal and the wolves should be "removed." Defenders of Wildlife, U.S. Fish and Wildlife Service, and other conservation groups filed an appeal to stop removal—more specifically extermination—of Yellowstone wolves. After much public debate and litigation, the U.S. Court of Appeals in Denver reversed the lower court's 1997 ruling against the wolves and declared in January 2000 that the Yellowstone wolves could remain in the park. This ruling followed another federal court decision to dismiss a lawsuit filed by the New Mexico Cattlegrowers Association requesting a halt in the fledgling Mexican wolf reintroduction program. Such recent court decisions signal a hopeful future for the three hundred wolves in this region.

Defenders of Wildlife President Rodger Schlickeisen said, "It's a new day for wolves in more ways than one. The Yellowstone wolves have been given a new lease on life and so has the principle that science, not politics, should guide wildlife restoration efforts in America."

In our regard for other predators, we are a species in conflict with ourselves. On one hand we restore, on the other, we revert to our fears and commit mass killing. Consider the polarities of state wildlife policy in Arizona and Alaska. In Alaska, wolves are still killed as they have been throughout the bloody history of the settling of the Old West. Even on the edge of a new century, there is no new frontier for Alaska's wolves.

Though an Alaskan public initiative in 1996 over-whelmingly passed by 63 percent of the voters to prohibit the aerial shooting of wolves, the Game Board and legislature is still committed to cruel wolf control by legislation undermining the public's increasingly pro-wolf stance.

In May 1999, the Alaska State Senate passed a bill, SB 74, subverting the public's initiative to ban same-day airborne shooting. State Senator Pete Kelley (R-Fairbanks) introduced SB

74 as a means to turn the existing ban into a vehicle for expanded wolf control. The Alaskan Senate vote not only conflicts with the 1996 citizen-enacted ban on same-day airborne wolf shooting, it also disregards a 1999 poll that shows 70 percent of Alaskans oppose any attempt to repeal the ban legislatively.

In September 1999, the Alaska State Legislature approved for a second time by a two-thirds majority SB 74, which now empowers the Alaska Department of Fish and Game—in addition to the Game Board—to kill wolves and bears from aircraft under a broad range of conditions. Basically, this latest legislative action overrides both the Alaskan citizens' successful initiative opposing airborne shooting as well as the Governor's veto of SB 74. It's business as usual with the Alaskan legislature—kill the predator!

Will Alaska continue its Old West extermination policies, even in the face of such public dissent? Will another tourism boycott be necessary to alert Alaska's state legislature to the dismay of the international public, as well as its own state-wide majority of voters?

Even now in Alaska it is legal to use bounty hunting, snares, traps, and sterilization to keep wolf populations low and game prey high. In Orwellian scope and doublespeak, this supposedly "non-lethal" strategy sterilizes alpha pairs. State agents swoop down from planes to snatch eight-to-ten-month old pups from packs and drop them hundreds of miles away to fend for themselves—alone in unfamiliar terrain with hostile hunters. Some wolf advocates actually say sterilization and relocation is worse than killing wolves, because it violates all biological and moral ethics, and is a kind of species slavery.

"What Alaska desperately needs is what the rest of the world is already discovering—a true conservation ethic," explains Dr. Vic Ballenberghe, a wildlife biologist with the U.S. Forest Service in Anchorage, who has studied wolves since the 1970s. Ballenberghe believes that decades of state wolf control programs have been "poor biology, often poor economics, and almost always poor public relations." He hopes for a new century that is "more in step with the rest of the world, where presently the dominant theme is to conserve wolves where they occur and restore them in areas where they are gone."

Then there is Arizona, which at first glance seems the polar opposite of Alaska's policy in our country's one-foot-forward and one-back dancing with wolves. Restoring the Mexican wolf, *El Lobo*, to its native habitat seemed an impossible task when retired grandmother Bobbie Holaday, founded Preserve Arizona's Wolves in 1988. She and the citizens of Arizona and New Mexico prevailed against hostile, organized cattle ranchers, a powerful right-wing legislature, and even a state bill to place a bounty on wolves.

In March 1998, three packs totaling eleven captive-bred Mexican wolves were released into the Blue Range of Arizona's Apache-Sitgreaves National Forest. Of these eleven Mexican gray wolves reintroduced, five adults and one pup are dead or presumed so by the U.S. Fish and Wildlife Service. Nancy Kaufman, director of USFS's Southwest region, states, "We're viewing this apparent shooting as an attempt to sabotage wolf recovery." Signaling that wolf restoration will indeed proceed, U.S. Department of Interior Bruce Babbitt journeyed to his native Arizona to help release two more female Mexican wolves. Babbitt stated firmly, "The Mexican gray wolf has come home and is here to stay." He added, "The reason we're releasing these two wolves is to send a message that this is public land.... Ninety percent of Americans support this [wolf-reintroduction] effort."

In Arizona, as in Alaska, there is a vocal minority who vehemently opposes and sabotages any wolf conservation. And as the support for restoring wolves grows in the national polls, so does the backlash from this Old West mindset. Says Arizona's Bobbie Holaday; "We are in a transition from the frontier/cowboy to a new ecological era; and we haven't quite built the bridge yet." Holaday tells the story of one Arizona family whose generations reveal the American history of human and wolves. It was Eugene Cleveland Holder, working for Arizona's Game and Fish Department who trapped the last wolf in Mogollan Rim, west of the White Mountains. Holder made that wolf skin into a stole for his sister, who never wore it. Eugene's grandson, Will Holder is now, along with his wife, one of the co-op farmers of Ervin's Natural Beef who supports the new policy of allowing no predators to be killed on their land—not mountain lions and certainly not wolves. In two generations, such change is encouraging.

What is also instructive about Arizona's reintroduction of wolves is that its wildlife programs are supported, not in the usual way by hunting licenses, but by a citizens' initiative that created a state lottery of $10 million per year for wildlife programs—from black-footed ferrets to California condors to Mexican wolves. Without the single-species game management of many states, the wildlife officials are free to study and support wildlife without a hunter's bias.

This may well be the trend for the future of wildlife management, now that less than 6 percent of the nation are active hunters. The U.S. Fish and Wildlife's Mexican Wolf Recovery Director, David R. Parsons, and wolf biologist Diane Boyd-Heger are quick to add that some hunters have also joined in the public support for wolf reintroduction. Citing a survey done by wildlife biologist Pat Tucker, Boyd-Heger explains, "In all the surveys of hunters on wolf reintroduction in every state from Arizona, New Mexico, Maine, Minnesota, Wisconsin, Wyoming, Montana, and Idaho, a majority of hunters favor wolf reintroduction."

The hunters' support echoes a strong groundswell of positive public reaction nationwide to wolf reintroduction. From surveys on wolf reintroduction conducted in upstate New York's Adirondacks National Park to Washington state's Olympic National Park—the support for wolf recovery is extremely high—84 percent in New England, 80 percent in New York and 76 percent in favor in the Adirondacks. And in Washington State, 62 percent polled favor reintroduction, with only 26 percent opposed. Interestingly enough, in this same poll, three-quarters of respondents believed "it is important that wolves are in the Northwest" not only "to balance the ecosystem" and because "it is the wolves' natural habitat," but also because there are moral and spiritual reasons to support wolf recovery.

In the 1997 Olympic Wolf Summit, state Representative Norm Dicks (D-WA) spoke out strongly for returning the wild wolf to its Northwest habitat. "We have an opportunity to correct an historic mistake," Dicks said. And in the Olympic Wolf Feasability Study released in March 1999 by U.S. Fish and

Wildlife Service, there is a positive first step toward reintroduction of the gray wolf to Washington's Olympic Peninsula.

History and our moral attitude toward other species are changing. The November 1998 "Restore the Wolf" conference in Seattle, Washington organized by Defenders of Wildlife was a welcome contrast to that 1993 Alaska Wolf Summit. For starters, we didn't have to sit on an ice rink surrounded by bleachers filled with angry hunters. In Seattle's conference, there were more than four hundred participants from across the country, more than half of them women. People from many diverse backgrounds shared a common interest in the wild wolf. At the hotel where the conference was held, even the employees joined in the excitement about wolf recovery. Several took their children out of school to see the many wolf exhibits and especially to meet two ambassador wolves from Colorado's Mission Wolf—captive-bred wolves who tour the country so that humans can come face-to-face with this creature so maligned by our myths.

As two schoolboys met their first wolf, Merlin, a young male with shiny black fur, they gazed into his intense yellow eyes and murmured, "Awesome...."

The boys' father, Paul Greenwood, a hotel employee, said, "This is about the future. Maybe someday my kids will even hear wolves howling again in the wild. And they won't be afraid."

"Yes," the boys' mother, Mary Greenwood, added as she proudly watched her oldest son reach both hands out, palms upward, to offer his shy friendship to the young black wolf. Merlin greeted the boy with a dignified gaze and an unexpected lick of the boy's entire face.

"That's Merlin's wolf way of memorizing or remembering you," Kent Weber, Director of Colorado's Mission Wolf told him.

"For sure, *we'll* all remember today and these beautiful wolves for the rest of our lives," said Mary. "It changes everything when you meet the real thing and not the big bad wolf of fairy tales."

Recently at a conference with the Center of the American West, I was on a panel to discuss new ways of looking at wildlife. The respected historian and McArthur Fellow Patricia Nelson Limerick, author of *The Legacy of Conquest: The Unbroken Past of the American West*, led the panel. In her inspiring speech, she remarked, "If somehow we could go back in history and interview our ancestors in the West from one hundred years ago, we might ask them, 'What is the most astonishing thing that has happened since your time?' What might they say? The most radical change is not the inventions such as automobiles or planes, nor the amazing technology we take for granted nowadays. The most astonishing fact to one of those early settlers or frontiersmen or farmer/ranchers would be this: That animals now have lawyers representing their rights. This advocacy would most amaze those of the Old West."

And yet the modern-day fact of lawyers, the public, and biologists lobbying for the return of the wild wolf to native habitats is not so very new; nor is it radical. Ask the Iroquois. It was the Iroquois Nation who would elect a person to sit in their formal council meetings as a representative of the wild wolves. It was the Iroquois who taught that any current decision must be made with the next seven generations in mind. Imagine a country in which our grandchildren hear again the howl of the wolves, a call to community, as did the First Peoples on this continent for thousands of years. In what is now upstate New York and western Pennsylvania, the Oneida Nation (one of the six nations of the Iroquois Confederacy) has a true story passed down many generations that illustrates a people who had learned to live in balance with the wild wolf. Paula Underwood, Oneida oral historian, recounts this learning story from her tribe's tradition. In "Who Speaks for Wolf," The People once forgot to consider the wolf while choosing their own territory,

> THEY SAW
>   That neither providing Wolf with food
>   nor driving him off
>   gave the People a life that was pleasing...
>
> THEY SAW, TOO,
>   That such a task would change the People:
>   that they would become Wolf Killers
>   A People who took life only to sustain their own
>   would become a People who took life
>   rather than move a little...
>
> IT DID NOT SEEM TO THEM
> THAT THEY WANTED TO BECOME SUCH A PEOPLE...

At last the Oneida decided to simply move themselves rather than intrude further on their "brother and sister," the wild wolf. From then on a member of the tribe was chosen to "ask the old, old question/to remind us of things/we do not yet see clearly enough to remember," to conclude:

> LET US NOW LEARN TO CONSIDER WOLF!

Another Native American voice raised to speak for the modern-day return of the wild wolf is Teresa Tsimmu Martino, author of *The Wolf, the Woman, the Wilderness* in which she tells the true story of raising and restoring an orphan wolf cub she named Mckenzie to the wild. Martino is the founder and director of a nonprofit organization called Wolftown on Vashon Island, Washington that does wolf and horse rescue.

Martino's remarkably vivid book draws poignant parallels between the brutal history of the wild wolf and her own Osage ancestors. It is a tale of dislocation and oppression and echoes the last century's systematic destruction of the wolves—a century in which our government placed a bounty not only on wolves, but also on Native peoples.

Martino, who is mixed blood Osage and Italian, mourns "losing my family stories and connection," and tells us, "My relatives on that side of the family are silent, except through the wolves." Martino's regard for wildlife echoes her Native American ancestors as she goes through the rigorous work of returning the gray wolf Mckenzie to the wild. "Wolves have a generosity of soul that makes humanity look uncivilized," Martino reminds us. She concludes that a new century of restoration will not only benefit the wolves, but humans as well. "If Mckenzie goes back, there is some part of me that will remain wild, too."

In speaking out for the return of the wild wolf, we can, all of us, shape an environmental history of the future; we can restore so much of what we and other species have lost in our headlong, rapacious claiming of territory that was never ours alone. A new century of conservation ethics will draw more from John Muir's visions than from the utilitarian and materialistic world view of the nineteenth and twentieth centuries. In *Trails: Toward a New Western History*, historian Donald Hall notes: "It is Muir who has turned out to be the most influential environmental reformer of his day, and it is his radical embrace of the non-human community that has gone out from the West to win a global audience."

Though we are in a volatile transition, the Old West extermination policies of wildlife management are dying. And as in any death throes, there is violence and backlash. Why should our wildlife continue to be seen only through the narrow sights of a gun? Or from the single-minded perspective of the agribusiness Farm Bureau that has also sued to stop wolf recovery in Idaho and in the Southwest? In this twenty-first century, our predator/prey relationship with other animals is evolving. We are beginning to recognize that as predator/hunters we have taken far more than we have restored.

Now those of us in the majority who do not use the wolf or their prey for our own needs, must work for peace for the wolves. Whether speaking out in management policies, in New West politics, or in the biological dialogues, we must open up the Old West backrooms. In the new millennium other species will not be seen as trophies to be taken, but allies to be restored. The animals will help us balance not only our complicated ecosystems—but also ourselves.

Noah's Ark Days

Sometimes I really do feel like road kill on the Information Highway—flooded by phones, faxes, mugged by FedEx messengers and my mailman. Recently I knew I was in trouble when I imagined a speaking engagement was really a getaway. En route to Boston with my laptop, I took my slim, assigned seat in that study-hall-in-the-sky. In the narrow plane, I plugged into my own private battery pack and computed across the continent. Around me passengers hooked up to portable phones, Game Boys, movie headsets, and Walkmans like so many dangling mid-air life support systems. We cruised, connected to the Earth by electricity, as if we believed we were safely tethered, still on-line.

The moment I stepped off the plane, my sponsor for the Boston Body/Soul Conference gripped me like a zealous tour guide. Whisked away along highways notorious for no signals and spontaneous merging, I checked into a friend's house, my nerves zinging, my eyes bloodshot, my breathing shallow—all the usual signs of information and sensory overload. I slept fitfully, dreaming that a team of highly paid surgeons was operating on my belly, installing a heavy, black extension cord to hook me up so that I might run more energy through this upgraded umbilical cord.

Next morning I awoke to something unexpected: a spacious quiet. My friend's huge 1920s house looked like an old French farm cottage with lush green vines crisscrossing the beige brick like veins. Calmly set in nine acres of autumn woods and bordering a monastery, the house glowed with reflected colors as all around red maples and amber oaks let go their leaves. Out my open window, I breathed in the sweet-rot perfume of fall trees and remembered that I, too, had a body with its own seasons, that it was time for me to turn inward and let go my work, even though I was here on business.

Gazing at the gloriously lit forest, I remembered that the reason leaves change colors is because the trees stop making chlorophyll so the true color of the leaves emerge when the green is no longer produced. I wondered, would I also grow more colorful and bright if I stopped producing—right in the middle of this business day?

I canceled all my appointments that day at the Body/Soul Conference; after all, wasn't the seminar supposed to be about union of physical and spiritual health? How could I teach others if my own body and soul were so stressed? There was a lesson in mindfulness and honesty that I needed to learn here. So I saw my friends off to work with an excuse about jet lag. I murmured under breath the real truth: That I wanted to unplug, disconnect, turn off, and imagine that like that neighboring monastery I was in full and profound retreat.

Several animal companions padded happily after me—three cats and an Australian shepherd whose tawny orange-and-white fur not only matched the sunroom's bright decor but also all the freckled Irish children's faces smiling out from every wall photo. Brady, the dog, Morris, the rotund tabby, the high-strung cat Sophie, and a gray feline crone called Kitty Kitty cozied up to me on the sun room's cushy couch. As I lay luxuriously gazing up through glass ceilings at the brilliant, swaying branches, the animals took up various lookout points on my body. Morris draped himself like a Davy Crockett hat over my head, his purring a meditative vibration inside my skull like cat plainchant. Sophie curled in a warm circle on my chest, while Kitty Kitty made a fur muff for my feet. And finally, with a contented sigh, Brady lay his long, stocky body alongside mine, his heart beating against my own slowed pulse.

Surrounded so by fur and the faithful, it was easy to imagine that this sun room sofa bed was its own tiny ark floating in luminous seas; and I, like Noah long ago when faced with a worldwide flood, was finding refuge and retreat with the animals. I thought of those contemplative brothers nearby in their monastery praying for the world; I thought of how it must have felt to float inside a wooden womb while the world was a deluge of water. With more animals than humans in that surviving ark, did Noah and his family learn humility before the wise, ancient eyes of the apes, the empathy of the elephants, the hibernating calm of reptiles and bears? Did that old ark rock and rest to the lullabies of great whales who dream and remember lost worlds?

Like natural Zen masters, animals spend their lives in the moment, fully present to the flow of life around them. I wonder, is our plugged-in, channel-surfing, shrinking attention span separating us from our own bodies, our Earth, our animal brethren, our center? I've read that the modern person is assailed by more information in one day's copy of *The New York Times* than our ancestors received in one lifetime. No wonder we humans are overwhelmed with the rising tide of the world's Flood of Info. And why not take to our own little arks and seek ancient animal companionship to help us survive? Resting with the animals, we gather from Noah's story: that companionable, interspecies communion is also a form of contemplation; that there are more profound ways of plugging in than our species has yet mastered. Electricity and modems are not our deepest connections. Real bonds are about body and Earth, fur and skin, and heartbeat and breathing.

Medical research has shown that petting one's cat or dog literally lowers the blood pressure. Animal companionship eases depression and aids those who are disabled or sick; prison inmates at risk have a reduced suicide rate when visited by animals; children do better in school if they have a pet; and elderly people who live with pets have longer life spans. Perhaps Noah's story is a survival tale for the twenty-first century—that letting go of the world to simply share a quiet day's shelter and retreat with other animals is a way to float upon the tidal waves of world-changing information without being overwhelmed.

Since that Noah's ark day of floating with the animals, I've decided to revise my daily practice. When I meditate, it will be lying down with my two cats and dog on my futon—my small, brave boat. Together we'll float above the raging floods. We'll reenact another ark in which the animals and humans still remembered how to talk together, to survive, to *be still and know*. And that is all the information we'll need.

Listening to the Sea Breathing

In British Columbia, on a remote, mist-shrouded island of thousand-year-old trees, OrcaLab researchers are listening to killer whales as they glide, leap, and greet other great gatherings of family clans, called superpods. For thirty years Dr. Paul Spong has been documenting these orcas; and he has been joined for the past twenty-two years by Helena Symonds, his partner both as researcher and spouse. They have stayed here on this largely uninhabited island studying the orcas who also make this cold, fertile Northwest Coast their seasonal home.

Using a sophisticated system of underwater hydrophones along the Johnstone Strait, Helena and Paul can record the complicated vocalizations of orca socializing—what Helena calls "sound sculptures" so intricate they require both a well-trained ear and computers to begin to fathom. Over the decades, they have learned to identify the signature calls and dialects of families and clans of northern resident orcas.

"Oh," Helena will say as she hears a high-pitched and rather sweet mewling like distant kittens, "here come the A36s." Headphones over her silver-blonde head, she sets several giant tape recorders spinning. She works in her weather-beaten lab on a day so foggy there is nothing to see but wet streaks of low-slung clouds. Yet it's hard to feel closed in when we are surrounded by exuberant and rapid-fire bursts—clicks and eerie arpeggios of ultrasound ranging far above our human hearing. "Remember, this is *live!*" Helena tells us with a wide, genial smile. "Just close your eyes and you'll hear the orcas better."

I put on guest headphones and listen to a wild symphony of orca calls, wondering what they are saying as clans greet and escort each other in the cold, deep waters along the Strait. Helena and Paul's approach is to listen, record, and learn to recognize orcas by their voices, in addition to the photo-documenting of their dorsal fins done by other sea-animal researchers. However, they acknowledge that humans may never be able to actually translate orca vocalizations into human speech.

These northern resident orcas are some of the most frequently studied of all marine mammals. And the killer whale is so beloved in the far Northwest that there is even an *Orca-FM* radio station devoted to airing the live whale vocalizations for Canadian residents. So when Northwesterners heard the news in the late fall of 1999 that orcas off Canadian and Washington State waters are the most heavily contaminated marine mammals in the world, they were stunned.

Canada became the first nation to officially declare their orcas as an endangered species and now there is a strong call in the United States to also list them. The problem is toxic PCBs in the waters. While these damaging chemicals were banned in Canada and the United States in the 1970s, it will take decades, perhaps even centuries, for the foul effects of these pollutants to disappear—if ever. Scientists from British Columbia, the United States, and Australia have documented that PCBs are still pouring into the world's waters from heavily industrialized Third World nations, as well as in Asia and Russia.

In northern Canada among the Inuit peoples, PCB levels are documented at ten times greater than in the general Canadian population. On Baffin Island nursing Inuit mothers must use powdered milk instead of breastfeeding their babies for fear of contaminating them. But in the wild waters, lactating orcas naturally purge the PCBs from their blubber every time they nurse which, in turn, poisons their offspring. There is now a 50 percent mortality rate for firstborn orca calves. And there has been a 15 percent crash in the southern orca populations of Washington since 1996.

In the late winter of 2000, there were reports of another troubling development for Northwest orcas. Puget Sound resident orcas—the L and K pods—were seen hunting for salmon as far south as Monterey Bay, California. To seek sustenance by traveling one thousand miles south, means the orcas are having difficulty finding food in their home waters in the Northwest. Before this unexpected sighting, Puget Sound orca pods were never known to travel even as far south as Oregon, much less south to waters off the coast of California. But Chinook salmon in Puget Sound have been listed under the Endangered Species Act, along with other depressed salmon stocks.

So, along with the discovery of toxic chemicals stored in their bodies, the orcas may now be starving in the Northwest. Some whale researchers, such as Kelly Balcomb-Bartok, who has studied orcas with Friday Harbor's Center for Whale Research for decades, wonders if our Puget Sound orcas will even return to the Northwest in the summer. "We don't know when they will come back north—if they do at all," Balcomb-Bartok told *The Sun* in Bremerton, Washington.

As international concern for the plight of these orcas grows and as a search for solutions intensifies, the subtle research at OrcaLab is even more critical. Orcas, like humans, are highly complex predators living at the top of their ocean habitat's food chain. If they are in trouble, it is a good indicator that land-dwelling mammals are endangered as well.

Now more than ever, the researchers at OrcaLab feel a sense of urgency and committed passion. Hydrophones strung among the islands of Parson, Flower, Cracroft, and Hanson relay vocalizations to broadcast speakers at OrcaLab. But it's not just in the laboratory when they listen to orcas. Twenty-four hours a day, from speakers in their cabin home rafters, their bedroom, moss-hung trees, and even the outdoor privy—Helena and Paul listen to orcas. In the middle of the night, throughout their days, whether she's baking bread or he's working on the fickle generator, when they hear orca vocalizations, both stop everything and rush to listen.

In 1998 I spent two days at Hanson Island's OrcaLab with Helena, Paul, and the orcas.

HELENA SYMONDS: What we do here is a lot of listening. I never particularly thought I was an auditory person. I was more visually oriented toward drawing and painting, yet my background is in theater, of all things. Suddenly, in coming here, I was placed in a world where listening is an important skill. Our ability to understand what we are listening to is our main research tool.

Each day, with the help of our hydrophone network, we try to track the whales within a forty-square-kilometer area. A lot of our work is at night when there are no possible complementary visual reports of the whales' whereabouts. We can discern from their vocalizations where the whales are, who they are gathering with, and what they're doing—whether they're resting, fishing, or socializing. It's really exciting. Remember, this is all live. Do you hear those calls coming through the speakers? That's the A36s.

BRENDA PETERSON: How can you tell them apart?

HS: It's largely a process of elimination. We have been following this group for many years now and they have become very familiar, so the task is not as difficult as it once was. When we started we learned to make gross distinctions. Within the main community of whales we study there are three main groups, called clans. Within each clan are a number of pods that share an acoustic tradition passed on from generation to generation through the orca mothers. So you say, okay, I'm hearing "A" clan calls and you know that in "A" clan there are nine pods. Even though these pods have several calls in common, each pod has a unique sound, and may even have particular calls that set them apart from the other pods. Once you have been able to identify the pod, the work becomes more complicated. Members of a pod are closely related, rather like an extended family, and they all make the same calls.

Hear that call? That's distinctive of the A36s. The A36s, one of three subpods that belong to the A1 pod, are Sophia, the orca mother, and her three sons, Cracroft, Plumper, and Kaikash. As Sophia's family does not always travel with the other two A1 subpods, we had to be able to distinguish her family's calls to keep track of their movements. Luckily, Sophia's family has visited this area quite often and we are able to tune our ears into their sounds. It's just a matter of becoming familiar with their voices.

BP: Just how important is family in the world of orcas?

HS: Very. An orca mother and her offspring, even adult sons, spend every day of their lives together. These groups are incredibly bonded; only death or capture will separate them. In 1990, we experienced a very clear illustration of the strength of those bonds. One night, late in November, we began to hear calls. As the night wore on we began to notice that many of the calls sounded very strange, agitated. We didn't realize until the morning that we were probably hearing the death of Eve, one of the older orca mothers. She and her two sons, Top Notch and Foster, had been seen the evening before. The next day her sons charged around Hanson Island very fast, first one direction, then the other. The mother was nowhere to be seen. We knew something was terribly wrong, because the three whales had never been apart. Eve's body was discovered ten days later.

When summer and the whales returned, Top Notch and Foster were missing. Some believe the sons had died without their mother. All of us were concerned. Finally, one day, the two brothers suddenly came swimming close to our shore. They joined the A36s, who are relatives but not their closest kin. The brothers at first seemed to keep a distance from the A36s. If the A36s swam on one shore the brothers swam on the opposite side. After awhile, the younger brother, Foster, began to befriend Sophia's oldest son, Cracroft. And soon after, the youthful antics of Kaikash, A36s' youngest, seemed to enliven Top Notch, who soon began to play too. It occurred to us that the brothers' alienation and grief were finally over. Not long afterward, the brothers rejoined their own family. After this experience I think we began to understand that the whole orca community is very significant, providing an extensive support system for each whale.

BP: Why are the females in orca society so important for the pod's survival?

HS: Once past infancy, female orcas may live a long life. The average life span is about fifty years, but many live longer. The oldest females in this community are about seventy-three years old; many are in their sixties and fifties. This longevity provides a great deal of stability in orca society. Young females grow up and establish their own families while still having the influence and wisdom of an older female at hand. The sons, who live much shorter lives on average, are able to remain with their mothers all or most of their lives. Each orca knows his or her place in the family, the pod, the community. They are very secure.

Orca societies are highly social, cooperative, and peaceful. Even after spending many years following and mapping the daily movements of the whales I am still impressed with how the whales coordinate their activities and how excited they seem to be with each other. We believe specific sub-pods may act as "hosts" to other visiting groups. Almost every season, Tsitika's group is the first to arrive here. As the summer progresses, Tsitika's family often wait on the outskirts of the area for new arriving groups, which they then escort into the area proper.

Early one evening in mid-August, many years ago, about thirty whales passed the Lab. The orange glow of the setting sun shone on their bodies as they spyhopped, slipping up from the surface in a sly, vertical twirl, and then they rushed northward. As the long summer twilight finally gave way to the night, a spectacular show of Northern Lights held us spellbound for what seemed like a long time. Just when we could hardly absorb any more wonders we started to hear the whales returning in the distance. Soon the ocean in front of the Lab was filled with the sounds of whales breathing and calls upon calls, a virtual mirror, as Paul put it, of the Northern Lights above us in the sky.

As the eighty whales moved together toward Johnstone Strait the August full moon rose and spilled its light into the remaining sky. Not hard to guess why I stay, is it?

BP: How is your work different from other whale research?

HS: Hanson Island has always been special. There has been a field research station here ever since Paul set up camp back in 1970, so we have been gathering data for nearly thirty years. I've been here for almost eighteen years. Interestingly, our method today is very similar to what it was in 1970. We decided back in the early 1980s we would only work from land. Several events contributed to that decision.

In September 1981, A24 gave birth to a calf right in Johnstone Strait. It is the only birth that has ever been witnessed in the wild. It was very exciting. A group of reporters happened to be in the area to cover the efforts to save the Tsitika Valley from logging, just happened to be returning from a visit to Robson Bight when the birth occurred. They, of course, photographed the new mom and the calf and the news was out! The next day the Strait was jammed with sightseers, ourselves included. Eventually, the boats made a complete circle around the new mom and her little one leaving the rest of the pod restlessly waiting outside.

It was a circus. There I was, sitting trapped in our boat with my young baby daughter in my arms, and there was A24, trapped out there with her baby, surrounded by so many people. I thought *there must be a better, a less invasive, way to study the whales.* That's when we decided to stop going out in boats and began to explore other ways to get information. We were fortunate to meet a local electronic wizard who expressed an interest in building remote transmitting systems. We began to experiment with these systems, trying to find the best locations that would allow us to listen to as wide an area as possible, including adjacent water-ways. We always had at least one hydrophone in front of the Lab before, but now suddenly we could hear where we couldn't see. We could follow the whales for hours.

Our hydrophone network is unique. Each year we record about a thousand hours of tape. We record every time we hear whales and this means we have to monitor twenty-four hours each day. Fortunately, we now have a lot of help from volunteers.

Each morning we listen to the tapes and try to retrace the whales' path from the day before. The summer months are busy and I am seriously sleep-deprived most of the time. I get very wrapped up in the whales and would rather be in the Lab than anywhere else. If I can't be there then I listen and keep track through the speakers in the house.

BP: You and your husband are very active in the movement to release and rehabilitate wild orcas captured and held in captive parks like Sea World. What is that research and work about?

HS: In the sixties and seventies almost seventy whales were captured from the Pacific Northwest. Most of the whales were taken from the Puget Sound area. Terrible damage was done. Many whales were killed outright during capture attempts. The pods involved in the captures are only now recovering three decades later. Of those seventy whales, only three have survived—

Corky, Yaka, and Lolita. Corky and Yaka were caught here in British Columbia in 1969. They are Northern Resident orcas, the same whales who visit our area each summer. Lolita is a Southern Resident and was caught a year later in Penn Cove, Washington. We feel that they need to be returned to their families as soon as possible. No one can say how much longer they will continue to live. Usually, orcas survive less than ten years in captivity. These three are nearing thirty years! They are old in captive terms but in the wild they would be young moms with probably a couple of kids each and many more years to live.

We are fighting to convince Sea World to free Corky. Anheuser Busch, the beer company, owns Sea World and they have huge resources, power, and influence. But we have managed to draw a lot of attention to Corky's plight and thousands of people have added their voices to the protest. We all believe Corky deserves a chance to come back home.

BP: If it were possible to get Sea World to release Corky after so much protest, it would set a precedent for the release of other captive orcas. Do you think it can be done successfully?

HS: Absolutely. We are not proposing that Corky just be dumped back into the ocean. She would be trained to catch live fish in her present tank and given extensive medical check-ups before she was brought to a halfway house near here, where she would have time to get adjusted before the whales arrived back for the summer. We would watch to make sure Corky and the other whales were ready before she was released. Corky has lots going for her. Her mother, Stripe, is still alive, as are several others who were in her pod when she was taken. She still makes the same calls as her family. She has survived losing seven babies, being attacked by another captive, and twenty-seven years of sterile concrete walls. Imagine that moment when she again feels her home waters surround her and hears her mother's voice.

BP: Do you think Corky's mother will remember her?

HS: Of course. Orcas have the second-largest brain of all animals, almost four times the size of a human brain and at least as complex. A good memory is certain. Corky was about four years old when she was caught. She has memories. When "Prime Time Live" played Corky's family's calls to her, she lay on the surface and shuddered. It was a powerful moment.

Orcas have to learn many skills and memorize huge, complex, geographical areas. Their range is hundreds of kilometers long, a maze of islands and waterways. All this knowledge is stored and retrieved with ease. When a calf is born, the pod takes the calf on a tour of their range to imprint knowledge of all the special areas. Perhaps that is why older individuals, especially long-living females, are important to the pod. Last summer, the oldest female—she is over seventy years old—toured this area with her son. As she swam along, every other whale came up to her, spent a few moments with her, and then moved away to allow her to pass. We have also seen other older females spend long hours with young whales, usually male, and often from a completely different pod.

BP: Do you think orcas are as aware of you and your family as you are of them?

HS: [laughing] I don't know that the orcas pay much attention to us. We're fairly secondary to them. I suspect it doesn't take a lot of energy on their part to take us in. They can easily do it and keep going. I think the most important thing for orcas is themselves, their families, their society.

There are times when I do wonder. One beautiful day in late fall we were heading back to the island and this young mom, Simoon, and her calf, Misty, were traveling toward us. We stopped and turned off the engine. Misty veered away from her mom and came close to the boat. As she swam past, in the clear water, she looked straight at us for a long moment before straightening up and swimming back to her mom. We all felt intuitively connected.

What always amazes me about orcas is how intensely focused they are despite disturbances. It is quite hard to gauge how boats are affecting the whales. Researchers keep getting confusing results when they observe boats and whales together. However, when we listen on the hydrophones, we get another impression about what is happening. We often hear the whales go quiet when a boat is approaching. They seem to be listening. After a while, they will echolocate, figure out where the boat is going, and then carry on.

BP: How do you think your intuitive feelings affect your under-standing of the whales?

HS: I think they fill in the gaps. There is so much we don't understand. Hydrophones, time, and experience all help, but so much remains hidden. After all, the ocean is not our natural home. We can only imagine. I think the total immersion, the constant presence of the whales in our lives has made us develop new awareness. I'm always thinking about what the whales are doing.

Sometimes, when it's late at night, when the sea is smooth and velvety under the moon and the whales are passing by, I just listen to the sea breathing. I believe staying here in one place, listening, not chasing, has changed me. We humans have so few models in our history of successful, peaceful coexistence within families and societies. Orcas have all of this. They can teach us—if we can only listen.

Great Blue

The balmy April morning I read about the Oklahoma City terrorist bombing I was trembling by the time I put down *The New York Times*. Old childhood images of being buried alive while bombs exploded overwhelmed me. I thought of those children who died in the blasts. Imagining their terror, I gave way to my own. After a childhood of 1960s duck-and-cover defense drills, that terror still feels so personal and physical. It's as if my psyche is hardwired to anticipate that at any minute the entire world will be savaged by apocalyptic, atomic flames.

I walked with my dog down to the beach. Ziggy looks like a black bear on a leash. When she loped along in her happy prance, I actually found myself smiling. How innocent she was of such human terror. But she wasn't numb. Every seagull, squirting anemone, or scuttling crab sent her canine instincts into an inquiry that was at once open, alert, and playful. Ziggy's animal presence, the shushing sound of waves off this inland sea, the early morning quiet—it all stilled my fears.

And then I saw something I will always remember: An Asian man stood on the beach, facing the water. Eyes closed, the man's hands poised palm upward in a gesture of reverence and surrender. He was murmuring in a low, gentle voice, perhaps a chant. I wondered if he was praying for the world.

Then five feet in front of him, with a whoosh of its wide, silver wings, a great blue heron landed on the wet sand. After studying the man intently, the bird turned trustingly away to face the sea. With mighty wings outstretched the great blue sunbathed in the bright breeze. This ancient bird was almost as tall as the meditating man. And I remembered hearing that in Asia the great blue heron is a divine messenger. Together the man and bird seemed to hold still a world careening into chaos.

At last I closed my eyes and my dog leaned trustingly against my legs. There were only the lulling waves, the man's musical chant, the great blue's serenity and trust in sun, wind, and human. I listened and wondered: Was this what the Taoist sages meant long ago when they revered water as the Way? They taught that one had great lessons to learn from a calm and happy spirit.

Animals often know this lesson before humans do. That great blue heron sensed that he was safe to fish and sunbathe so close in front of a meditating man. As I witnessed the serene, self-possession of both human and great blue, my whole body rested. At that moment, I realized that just because a bomb blew up in Oklahoma City, my own body did not have to shut down or automatically go on "red alert." Entering the chaos was an exploitation of the body, as well as of the Earth. Instead, I could simply witness the specter of that devastation. Then with love and compassion, I could detach from the fear and take myself down to the beach to pray; pray for my species, for other animals, and for the world.

This silent witnessing is far from denial; it is acceptance of the pain, and then allowing other balancing stories and connections. If the connections we make are only within our own species, we will miss the chance to discover other, what David Abrams calls, "more-than-human" teachers. I believe that between that great blue heron and the man on the beach there was a connection that made their presence and perhaps prayers more powerful than what we might do alone.

While we have information enough to overwhelm any species, we rarely have cultivated calm—the kind of animal stillness and scrutiny that is the opposite of the fight-or-flight stimulus. The serpent coils in surrender to sunlight on a steaming stone; the feline rests and contemplates a spacious savanna; the patience of the cow with her endless cud. These animal images of quietude and being are opposed to the incessant business and doing so valued by our species. And yet it is in just such meditative moments we often see the world most clearly.

In *Back to Beginnings: Reflections on the Tao*, the ancient Taoist writer Huanchu Daoren writes, "Best be very calm yet radiantly alert... When people are in positions of power and occupy important offices, their behavior should be strict and clear, while their state of mind should be gentle and easy." In Stephen Mitchell's translation of the *Tao Te Ching*, he quotes

Lao Tzu as saying, "We might seek a path that is radiant but easy on the eyes."

It is interesting to note that the words *radiant* and *radiate* come from the same root word, which has to do with a radius or center. "Radiant" describes bright, often illuminating, rays of light and "radiate" is when those rays penetrate us for the purpose of healing—or in the case of atomic weapons, self-destruction. Since the first penetrating rays of atomic light mid-twentieth century, we have all been terribly radiated, some physically and all psychologically. Can we in a new century change that pain and terror into radiance and true illumination that is indeed "easy on the eyes," as well as the body?

The 1995 Oklahoma City bombing brought home to our American ground a glimpse of what it must have been like for Hiroshima or Nagasaki. The U.S. decision to drop atomic bombs in 1945, in retrospect, has been revealed to be the result of political bureaucratic momentum, and wartime fear. The decisions being made today are also too often done in the midst of terror or misinformation. If we can ask our leaders to balance their action with reflection, their fear with calm—we may well do more than avoid the atomic blasts that have haunted us for so long. We may instead usher in the twenty-first century in which the citizenry rewards calm, considered action rather than panicked aggression; the trigger-happy images of Americans that were so perfectly summed up in the 1960s by the Rand Corporation's reference to apocalypse as "war-gasm."

The original Greek meaning of the word *apokalypsis* is "revelation." And certainly we've all witnessed in some form the shocking flash of light from an atomic bomb—but have we yet been truly illuminated by this brilliant light? While the prospect of nuclear war has forced us into some well-needed restraint in terms of starting WWIII, it has not taught us how to heal the terror we are nursed like toxic mother's milk. Post Cold War we have transferred our nuclear terror into new end-of-the-world scenarios: environmental apocalypse, sexual and bacterial plagues, national and international terrorism.

As the children of the Cold War mature into a new century and assume the mantle of power left us by a post-World War II, Depression era, bomb-dropping past generation, can we now as elders find some calm and clarity and self-mastery?

Acknowledging this new century's need for self-restraint and self-knowledge in the era of atomic weapons, Andrew Bard Schmookler, author of *Debating the Good Society: A Quest to Bridge America's Moral Divide*, urges that "along with our newly achieved godlike powers, our kind is now challenged for its very survival to arrive at new images of godliness. Not just the possession of power, but its restrained use. Not just bestriding the world in a posture of mighty dominance, but fitting in and aligning oneself with a larger order that serves life."

As I watched the man and the great blue heron on the beach that day of the Oklahoma City terrorist bombing, I vowed to spend the second half of my life studying self-mastery, controlling my own fears, and aligning my body and soul with serving life. I reminded myself that the Chinese goddess of compassion Kuan Yin is said to cry one perfect tear when faced with tragedy. She is also armed with forty-two weapons of self-defense to perform her compassionate, calm work in the world. I'm sure that one of her tools is detached love.

The great blue heron, the meditating man, the gently soothing waves taught me how to respond to this terrible act of terrorism—a quiet vigil with man, bird, water, and dog. So I stood back on the beach, surrounded by gnarled, resting driftwood and bowed my own head.

Be with us, I asked of all that is holy, of all the guardians of this great blue world, spinning in meditative space. *Abide with us. Teach us peace and stillness in the midst of terror. And may we serve all life.*

At last I raised my head. The great blue heron, turned and looked beyond the man to Ziggy and myself; so tall on those crane-legs, so graceful with the keen yellow eye and black-crowned feather cap. The meditating man gave the great bird a deep slow bow—a gesture at once grateful and reverent. Without warning, with one mighty flap of ancient wings, the bird lifted up from the waves, cawing. The call of a dinosaur bird who had escaped extinction, who circled above us once, and then was gone—carrying the souls of our children into the great blue.

OTHER BOOKS BY BRENDA PETERSON

NOVELS —

Duck and Cover; HarperCollins, 1991. *New York Times* Notable Book of the Year.

Becoming the Enemy; Graywolf, 1988.

River of Light; Alfred A. Knopf, 1978; paperback edition, Graywolf, 1987.

NONFICTION —

Build Me an Ark: A Life with Animals; W. W. Norton & Company, 2001.
A memoir.

The Sweet Breathing of Plants: Women Writing on the Green World;
Farrar, Straus, & Giroux, 2001. Anthology co-edited with Linda Hogan.

Sightings: The Many Mysterious Worlds of the Gray Whale;
National Geographic Books, 2002.

Intimate Nature: The Bond Between Women and Animals; Ballantine, 1997.
Anthology co-edited with Linda Hogan and Deena Metzger.

Pacific Northwest: Land of Light and Water; Sasquatch Books, 1998.
Text by Brenda Peterson and photographs by Art Wolfe.

Nature and Other Mothers; HarperCollins, 1992; paperback edition,
Ballantine, 1995.

Sister Stories; Viking, 1996; paperback edition, Penguin 1997.
Two-volume audiocassette based on the book performed by author,
Sounds True, 1996.

Living by Water; Alaska Northwest, 1990; paperback edition, Ballantine,
1994. America Library Association Editor's Choice Award.

Singing to the Sound is the long-awaited sequel to Brenda Peterson's popular classic *Living by Water* first published in 1990. From her two decades on the shores of Puget Sound, Peterson now advances her "love song for a region" into a new century in which the West is leading and shaping environmental ethics worldwide. An acclaimed nature writer, Peterson's literate, lyrical writing moves from stately reporting to memoir.

L. A. Henderson

Singing to the Sound reveals darker and more troubled waters—from the Makah whale hunt to the feared extinction of Northwest salmon. Peterson also offers subtle solutions and visions of future environmental restoration and healing. Peterson's writing moves from love song to prophesy, from the way things are to a vision of what they might be.

Brenda Peterson is the author of three novels, one of which, *Duck and Cover*, was selected by *The New York Times* as a "Notable Book of the Year." Her recent works of nonfiction include her memoir, *Build Me an Ark: A Life with Animals.* She has co-edited with Linda Hogan two highly acclaimed anthologies; the groundbreaking *Intimate Nature: The Bond Between Women and Animals* and *The Sweet Breathing of Plants.* Upcoming work by Peterson includes *Sightings; The Many Mysterious Worlds of the Gray Whale* (National Geographic, 2002), co-authored with Linda Hogan.

Peterson lives in Seattle on the shores of Puget Sound with her beloved cat, Isabel.

Other Books on Animals from NewSage Press

NewSage Press has published several titles related to animals. We hope these books will inspire humanity towards a more compassionate and respectful treatment of all living beings.

Conversations with Animals: Cherished Messages and Memories as Told by an Animal Communicator
by Lydia Hiby with Bonnie Weintraub

Blessing the Bridge: What Animals Teach Us About Death, Dying, and Beyond
by Rita M. Reynolds

Unforgettable Mutts: Pure of Heart Not of Breed
by Karen Derrico

Three Cats, Two Dogs, One Journey Through Multiple Pet Loss
by David Congalton

When Your Pet Outlives You: Protecting Animal Companions After You Die
by David Congalton and Charlotte Alexander (*available May 2002*)

Food Pets Die For: Shocking Facts About Pet Food
by Ann N. Martin

Protect Your Pet: More Shocking Facts
by Ann N. Martin

Dancer on the Grass: True Stories About Horses and People
by Teresa Tsimmu Martino

The Wolf, the Woman, the Wilderness: A True Story of Returning Home
by Teresa Tsimmu Martino

NEWSAGE PRESS

For a catalog contact NewSage Press
PO Box 607, Troutdale, OR 97060-0607
www.newsagepress.com
Email: info@newsagepress.com
Phone Toll Free: 877-695-2211 or 503-695-2211
Fax: 503-695-5406

Distributed to bookstores by Publishers Group West:
800-788-3123 (U.S.) or 416-934-9900 (Canada)